WHITE HOT AND RED
A Vietnam Diary

Vincent Carmack

ISBN: 1-4196-9225-9
ISBN-13: 9781419692253

Visit www.booksurge.com to order additional copies.

A SPECIAL THANKS TO:

Greg Rainwater
John Canfield
Rod Lawson
Cheryl and Heather Healy

PREFACE

The reader may wonder how after forty-one years I was able to recall in detail the events that took place during my time in South Vietnam. To recall events in detail I carried a diary to record the things I saw, the things I did and most of all the things I felt. So this is my story, my memories and my thoughts.

Contrary to belief about war it's not a place of excitement or glamour, but a place of horror, long periods of time alone and thinking, places of fear, of bone weary tiredness, thirst, hunger and frustration. You lived and survived in the rain, mud, dirt, heat, sweat and you could only wonder why you were there at all. There were no cameras, glamour or heroics as the movies portray, there is only you, doing what you have to do, simply because you're there. When these young Marines got shot, they died. They were carried off the battlefield with their heads dangling, bobbing up and down like a spring. Some died slowly clutching the stub of an arm or leg and staring in unbelief that it happened. Some of them saw me watching helplessly as their lives spilled out onto the ground. Their hopes and dreams dimming into unconsciousness and they were gone. I watched as they died.

The names of the people in this book have been changed to protect the families of those who have already lived through the horrors of war. Others who were there have their own story with different experiences. This is what I remember as my time "in country." Now, go back in time to 1966, to a war torn country called South Vietnam and look through the eyes of a naive eighteen year old Marine.

WHITE HOT AND RED
A Vietnam Diary

**Dedicated to my Grandbabies,
Brandon, Brandi, Madison**

May they never know the horror of War

For all who have earned and worn
the eagle, globe, and anchor, the Marine Corps

CHAPTER 1

THE BEGINNING

Behaviorism, we are the product of our environment whether for good or for evil. These words still ring in my ears even after forty one years. The words came from my English teacher Mr. Strickland on the last day of my senior year when I told him I was dropping out of high school and that I had joined the Marine Corps. I didn't know then the meaning behind those words, but I would find out with the passing of time.

It was the beginning of March 1966 and the senior class of Mountlake Terrace High was getting ready to finish their last quarter of high school. Knowing that I was two credits short of graduating I had decided to hell with it. I had been working since I was thirteen years old in Seattle, six hours a day, six days a week trying to go to school at the same time. I didn't know what a summer break was.

My mother had been married six times and although I had three brothers and one sister, none of us had the same Father except with the possibility of the youngest brother and sister. Strange, how we all ended up with the same last name. My Mother must have liked it. I hated her for a long time because of what she had done with her life. There was never enough money to pay the bills and sometimes no food in the house. We had been on and off welfare for years. My Mother was only fourteen when she gave birth to my older brother Terry and had just turned sixteen when she had me. She would hang around the Navy bases like Navy Yard City Bremerton Washington where I was born and The Naval Air Station on Whidbey Island Washington. She was there to meet sailors that she could drag home for the weekend. My Brother was eight and I was six and often we would be alone all weekend, day and night.

Mother would show up sometimes in the middle of night with some sailor who in the morning, would come out of her bed room in his boxer shorts looking for the bathroom. They would always ask me or my brother how we were doing and sometimes ask us our names. Some of them were cool guys and would show me their tattoos'. Some of them didn't want to be bothered with kids. They were just there waiting to leave with my Mom for the night and or for a great weekend. I do have to admit that when some of them shacked with her for a few weeks we had food to eat and the rent got paid.

There was one sailor who was a real bastard and I hated him. To this day I still do. I often wish that I would run into him someday so that I could beat the hell out of him. That's kind of funny though because he would be (how old?) I hated him because he was always hitting my brother and me when he got drunk which was most of the time. I couldn't understand how my Mother could allow someone to beat her kids over nothing, again and again. I still remember to this day something that happened that I still have nightmares about. It was on a Friday night when I was seven years old. My brother was staying over night with a friend of his. I was alone for the night. I got kind of scared being alone so I let my dog in the house. His name was Old Yellow sort of like the movie Old Yeller. My Mom and this bastard had a fight as they usually did when they both got drunk. He took off for our house and left her at the dance hall. I was told by this ass that I wasn't supposed to have my dog in the house. He hated cats and dogs. I was sitting on the couch watching TV when he tried to open the door, of course it was locked. He started pounding on it yelling to let him in. For a moment I just froze. Then I realized that I had to get Yellow out the back door so he wouldn't get mad and start hitting me. By the time I got there he had already gone around the house to the back door. He was standing there when I opened it. He started yelling at me for not unlocking the front door, but stopped in the middle of yelling when he saw Old Yellow. He said "so you don't want to listen to me about that dam dog." Well this is it. He turned and went in to the pantry grabbed a hammer and started to hit Yellow with it. I tried to stop him but he pushed me across the kitchen floor into the cabinet and I fell hitting my head. By then Yellow was trying to protect me, but he hit Yellow in the head with the hammer. Yellow tried to crawl under the kitchen table but the asshole hit him again. It was too late to stop him. Yellow laid there dying on my lap. Blood poured out over me and onto the floor while this bastard went to bed. I cried and cried until I passed out from hitting my head so hard. My Mother finally came home around two o'clock in the morning with a girl friend of hers. When she saw me she started screaming what is going on! When I told her she grabbed a big knife out of the drawer and run into the bed room. That would be the last time I would see the bastard. He ran out of the house in his boxer shorts. That was the first time she had ever protected me from him.

There were always prostitute girl friends of my Moms hanging around the house. Sometimes they would walk around with their cloths off with their boobs hanging out. I guess if I knew then what I know now, maybe I would have enjoyed it. But at five, six and seven years old I was into cartoons.

When I was seven and a half my Mom sold me to her Aunt and Uncle that lived in Cobalt Idaho. This was the same Aunt that my Grandmother gave her youngest daughter (my mom's sister) to when she was just a baby. For years I thought the girl was my cousin, but actually she's my Aunt. That jumped out of the bag after my Grandmother died. I was sold to them because he worked in the coal mines and didn't come home until late at night. They needed someone to carry the water from the steam to the two room cabin they lived in as well as cutting the wood for the stove for heating and cooking. That's when I learned to cook because this woman would only cook for herself and the girl. Basically I was a slave. There was no love from them to me. Just love for the girl who I just started talking to again two years ago. She still lives in Idaho. She was a real jerk when we were kids, but has told me that she is sorry now, over and over again for the way she and her Mom and Dad treated me.

One of the games they liked to play when she did cook something for all of us was having me take food from the table and then tell me I was a hog. Put it back she would say. If I put back to much I got hit in the face and told to take more. This would go on and on until my mouth started bleeding and the blood dropped on my food. She made me eat it anyway. It took me years to get over seeing ketchup on food without making me sick.

When the woman caught cancer she became bed ridden and the Uncle didn't want me around, so he shipped me back to Seattle on a train from Salmon Idaho. I was nine years old. That was two years of hell I was glad to put behind me.

The hell started again however when I got to Seattle. My Grandmother (my Mom's Mother) hated me. So when I showed up in Seattle she made sure she wasn't there to meet me on time. I waited for hours and when she did arrive she told me that she thought she was rid of me forever. I found out years later that she hated my real Father because she wanted to have an affair with him and he didn't want anything to do with it. I don't know if it's the truth or not. My Grandmother was thirteen when she had my Mother, so who knows. The whole family was so fucked up it was no surprise that I joined the Marine Corps, not only because I had a very low self-esteem, but also we needed the money. There were still three small children in the house. I was seventeen and lied about my age to enlist. During the Vietnam War the Marines wanted bodies so no one bothered to ask any questions.

CHAPTER 2

BOOT CAMP

On the day I left to go to boot camp it was raining and cold outside. The house was quiet with very little light coming through the windows. I can still remember standing at the window thinking about a girl I had just met two days before on the beach. A friend of mine from school was going to the beach with his girl friend and she was bringing along her cousin, so I guess I was suppose to be a blind date. How odd that seems to me now. The first time I saw her I thought she was the most beautiful thing on the face of the earth. I had never had a girl friend before due to my job and having little money didn't help. There was that occasional kiss here and there with the neighborhood girls, but never anything else. We spent the next two days together talking, kissing, holding hands and listening to music. To this day I don't really know why she bothered with me, unless it was because I was going in the Marine Corps and it made her feel good to have a boy friend in the service. I didn't touch her sexually even though she tried hard to get me to. Maybe she thought I was a nice guy for not trying anything. I was still a virgin and I didn't smoke, swear, or drink at that time. I knew very little about girls and when I heard guys talking about sex I got very confused.

The night before leaving for boot camp we had said our goodbyes and promised to write to one another while I was away. Just then a loud noise outside brought me back to my reality. I realized that I had been standing there with all this running through my head. When I looked out the window to see what it was, I saw my friend Duane. He was coming down the dirt road to pick me up in his old green Buick. It had smoke coming out of the back and was back firing. At least he had a car, I only had two feet. It was time to go and as I turned around to pick up my suitcase I heard my mother ask me, weren't you going to tell me goodbye? She turned on the lamp and when I saw the look on her face I started to get choked up. Why did her life have to be such a mess! I walked over to her gave her a hug and told her I loved her. I picked up my suitcase and opened the door just as Duane was getting ready to knock. As we drove down the driveway I caught just a glimpse of my Mother watching the car from the window. I wondered being so young at the time if I would ever see her again. I think probably every kid feels that way when they leave home for the first time. Duane dropped me off at the bus depot where I was to report to a military desk. We hugged each other without even thinking about it. Had I known at the time that it would be last time I would ever see him, I would have told him I loved him like a brother. We had known each other since junior high school and when we grew up we wanted to go on the road down route 66 just like the television show. If he had a dollar in his pocket he would say we both got fifty-cent where do we eat. Six months after I got to Vietnam his mom wrote to me. I knew that Duane had gotten drafted into the Army because I received a letter from him saying "guess what, I've been drafted". He was a gunner on a chopper hit by a NVA rocket. Everyone along with him was killed.

As I entered the bus depot I saw a large group of boys about my age standing next to a wall. There were a couple of men wearing uniforms standing in front of them taking the bus tickets out of their hands. As I walked up to one of them he said give me your name and stand with your back to the wall. Shut up until I tell you to talk. My name was the last thing I said for an hour. We loaded the bus and pulled out on the way to the airport. No one said a word until we got there. Two hours later I was on my way to San Diego California aboard United Airlines. The trip down seemed like it took forever. I was getting real scared and started to wish I were back home again. I had to choke back my tears, that's all I needed was for someone to see me crying for his mommy. After all I was going to be a Marine. Finally the plane touched down in California. We loaded onto the Marine Corp buses and were on our way to the Marine Corps Recruit Depot (MCRD.) I fell asleep along the way. I was so tired from worry and just thinking too much. I'm glad now I fell asleep, I needed it.

I woke up with someone yelling at the side door of the bus. The yelling was coming out of the biggest, meanest, man I had ever seen. He was your worst nightmare. There would be no sleeping tonight. Just for a second everyone froze in place not having a clue what he was saying. When he grabbed a guy and threw him off the bus we all got the message. Forty guys all trying to get off the bus at the same time. It must have been funny to watch. Later I would laugh about it, but not for a long time after boot camp. We stood on little yellow foot prints while this monster from hell Drill Instructor went up and down hitting people and yelling at the top of his lungs.

I got hit a couple of times during my training. Once was when the drill instructor was trying to fit me with a gas mask. It was a small size. After beating it on my face a few times he looked at it and blamed me for having a medium face. My face hurt but I almost smiled because of the way he blamed it on me. The second time was when my arm got tired holding up my rifle for twenty minutes, I lowered my shoulder just a little, but that's all it took. Some of the other guys really went through hell. We had our heads shaved, our clothes taken away and given a baggy uniform. I never dressed so fast in my life. He marched us around and around for two hours and then led us back to the huts where my home would be for eight weeks. He locked us in saying that no one goes over the wall on my watch. What wall? What the hell was he talking about? That was a long night for a lot of guys. I pounded on my head for a while and then thought about why I had joined the Marines. I wanted someday to be able to walk with my head up and not feel like a dirt bag. Somewhere in the night I fell asleep, but it seemed only minutes before the door slammed open. In came the boogie man throwing trash cans all around the hut.

First thing in the morning you were led to the bath house for a shit, shower and shave whether you needed it or not. Then it was on to the chow hall to get your morning meal. The food was great and you could have all you wanted if you weren't over weight. I was only one hundred and fifty pounds so he made me take allot more food than I wanted. In the Marine Corps you eat everything on your plate. Then it was on to physical training for most of the day. Each day was pretty much the same thing day after day, for the first couple of weeks. After that there was still allot of physical training but we were starting to get into what the Marines were all about. The pride, the history of the Marine Corps from 1775 all the way to 1966. We learned hand to hand combat as well how to handle weapons of various sorts. By my sixth week of training I was really getting in shape and I was proud. I knew I was going to make it. The best way to describe boot camp would be to have people watch the movie, Full Metal Jacket. The day I graduated from boot camp no family or friends were there to see it. I walked around watching some of the other guys with their families and it hurt for a while. But now I was a Marine and it was time I started acting like one. After all, tomorrow I was being shipped to my first assigned camp for four weeks of extensive training on combat strategies, jungle survival and brain washing tactics.

I had requested Recon, the Special Forces of the Marine Corps. I wanted those wings more than anything else in the world. I had scored high on most of my exams and had qualified as a rifle expert and as a sharp shooter with the 45 caliber. All I needed now was to make the height and weight restrictions. I remember the day I found out that I had made the list, I was so happy. I even took liberty that weekend. That was the first time that I left the base since arriving there. Most of my money was being sent home to my Mother to help out. Besides I was doing allot of letter writing to keep myself busy. Lana the girl I left back at home was writing me every week. I was really getting to know her, maybe even love her. At the end of my six week Recon training, which was the hardest physical training I had ever gone through, it was time to be presented with my wings. How proud I was of myself.

I still have the scars from where they pinned (pushed) them into my bare chest. One more day and it would be time to go home on leave. My leave had to be cut short to fifteen days because of the further training I needed in Recon. That training would be on the island of Okinawa in the South Pacific.

'

CHAPTER 3

FIRST LOVE

I can still remember looking out the window of the plane as it approached Seattle Tacoma airport and how strange I felt not seeing Washington State for so long. I thought about Lana and wondered if she really did feel the way she said she did in her letters. I wondered when I got off the plane if she would be there waiting for me. When the plane touched down my heart started pounding, I thought it would jump right out of my chest. I was real proud of my uniform, my private first class stripe and most of all my wings. As I disembarked from the plane I didn't see anyone around. After a few moments a man my Mother had been working with at a dry cleaners shop, walked over and said hey Marine, need a ride? I said yes sir thank you. I kept looking around for Lana but she wasn't there. Riding back to my Mother's house I wondered if I gave Lana the wrong date of when I was coming home. Yes that was it. I must have given her the wrong date. I thought to myself I should have called her before I left California. It had been so long since I had been away I didn't notice that we were going out of our way back to the house. Finally he asked me if I had a problem with him stopping by the shop to pick something up. I told him that was ok with me. I wasn't really in a hurry anymore. He asked me to come in with him because he had a couple of big boxes to carry and would I mine helping him. He went in first, turned around and said, welcome home Vince. As I looked around the room I saw my two younger bothers, my sister, my Mother and my Aunt Helen, but no one else except a few friends of my Mothers. It must have only been a moment in time, but seemed like a week before out of the back room came Lana. Her long blonde hair rested on her shoulders and her dark brown eyes were shining like stars. She was more beautiful than I had remembered. That night back at my Mother's house we talked all night, she fell asleep on my lap for a couple of hours. I sat there looking down at her sleeping for a long time. I couldn't believe that I had really found someone who loved me. Finally I fell asleep. About three-o'clock in the morning she had to go home. I walked her out to her car and watched as she drove away. I kept watching her car until her tail lights faded into the dark. I really thought I was in love with her at the time and maybe I was, but something told me that it would be a long time, before I could give anyone love. I was used to being rejected allot as a child and had learned to keep my true feelings inside.

The next day and everyday we saw one another, we had fun talking and laughing and of course making out. Although I came close a couple of times I never made love to her, in fact I only touched her left breast once in all the time I knew her. Maybe that's why she wrote me a Dear John letter, while I was in Vietnam. I remember the first time I came even close to doing anything with her was on my third day home. I had a couple of friends over to have a few drinks. I didn't drink so I had no idea what was going to happen next. After what seemed to be a gallon of whiskey but more likely two drinks, I was loaded. Lana helped me out to her car. I didn't feel very well so

I kept my head out the window so that I wouldn't get sick. She drove down to Martha Lake and helped me get to the dock. Then she took her clothes off. She looked so beautiful standing there naked in the moon light. She tried to help me get my clothes off but I was so drunk I couldn't stand up. She got so mad at me she pushed me off the dock into the water. There's nothing like cold ice water to bring your ass back too earth. She jumped in after she pushed me to make sure I didn't drown. She helped me back to shore and we laid there just for a minute looking up at the stars. She was holding on to me so tight, if only I hadn't drunk so much she would have been my first. On the night before I had to leave for California. Her mom said I could stay the night so we would have more time together. Of course that meant different rooms. Her mom fixed us dinner with all the trimmings including wine. My plane wasn't leaving until 2 pm the next day, so we stayed up until 2 am and then went to bed. I had just fallen asleep when I felt something on the foot of the bed. It was Lana. She was climbing up to me. My heart started to pound so hard I thought the house would shake. She put her face next to mine and said I love you, please make love to me. She was dressed in a white short night gown that went down just to her navel and she had on white lace panties. My God she was driving me crazy. She kissed me on the chest and then on the neck and then gave me a lip lock like I had never had before. She finished her kiss by biting my lower lip. My mind was racing faster than lightening and I couldn't help but wonder if all girls do this at age seventeen. All of a sudden there was a knock on the bedroom door. It was her Father. Lana got up opened the door and told her Father that I had nothing to do with this. Her father said, I know. You're in his room, he's not in your's. Go to bed young lady we will talk in the morning.

When morning came I got dressed and went into the kitchen. I thought I was a dead man. I may have been a Marine but her Father stood six foot four inches and was in really great shape and even though he was a much older man. He wasn't too old to kick my ass. Besides, I had it coming. Lana wasn't there; her mom told me that she had asked her husband to take Lana out to breakfast so that she could get to know me better. She put some bacon in a pan on the stove, picked up her coffee cup and sat down next to me. She began by telling me she thought I looked like a fine young man and that if some day I were to be her son in-law she would be proud to have me. She said what I'm going to tell you may hurt you, but in time you will understand. You are so young and so is my daughter. You really can't begin to understand what love is all about. She paused for moment and then she asked if she could tell me a story. She started by telling me, you know my husband is not my first husband, he's my second. My first husband was killed in WWII. So was my brother. I still blame myself for my brother's death. I just had to be married no matter what. I was young and didn't want to wait until he came home. My husband was a Marine, young and handsome just like you. His company was pinned down on a beach by the Japanese. My brother was in the Navy and knowing that his brother in-law was still on the beach pinned down, he volunteered to go in and help get the Marines off the beach. The Navy got them off the beach but not without a loss of life. Both my husband and my brother were killed. All of this because, I just had to be married. Maybe my brother would have gone in anyway, but I will never know. What I'm trying to tell you is that I don't want you to be worrying about Lana while you're in Vietnam. You will have enough to worry about. I hope my daughter will wait for you, but she is so young and the young do stupid things. Lana returned with her Father about twenty minutes later. She looked at me with a strange look wondering what her mom had said to me. All I told her was that her mom was a great lady and that she should be very happy to have her for a Mother. Later that afternoon Lana drove me to the airport and waited until I boarded the plane. Later she would write that she waited until the plane was out of sight before she left. She was crying really hard and I almost started doing it myself. I kissed her one last time and walked down the ramp to the plane. I looked back three or four times. I even walked back just once to kiss your soft lips one more time. That would be the last time I would ever see her. I often wonder what if we had gotten married. I would have loved having a daughter just as beautiful as she was. But I guess a daughter is out of the question now. I do have two boys that I love very much. I also have a wonderful and beautiful daughter in-law, so in a way, I do have a daughter. I was married but now divorced. My sons have grown up and left home. I don't own a home, but I live with a beautiful and wonderful lady who makes her home feel like it's ours. She makes my life worth living.

Chapter 4

Radio School

Two and a half hours later my plane touched down in San Francisco. I looked at my orders. I was to report to Treasure Island for three days of training on communications. I was to receive training on the PRC 25 radio used in Vietnam. The training wasn't easy but I got through it. Then it would be back to Camp Pendleton 3rd Marine Recon Battalion for more training. My first night at Treasure Island was my first experience with war. I was going to hit the sack and because of the early morning rises in the in Corps I got use to taking my showers at night. When I stepped into the shower I was shocked by what I saw. There was a Marine standing with his back to me with his head under the shower head. There were deep dark holes from his neck down to his thighs, mostly on his lower back and butt. I tried not to stare, but I had never seen anything like that before. Later on that night I asked one of the other guys if he knew what all those scars were from. He said those are shrapnel wounds from a mortar round. I could feel the blood rush through my body. I thought about how I first felt when I was told I was going to Nam. It was the same feeling. I laid there thinking about it for a long time. I told myself that nothing like that could ever happen to me. That's the night I started to keep a diary.

I finished my three days of training at radio school and reported to Camp Pendleton. I had twenty-four hours left until I would be on my way to Okinawa to finish my Recon training. I spent most of it writing letters, calling home and calling Lana. We talked allot about what we were going to do when I got back home. I remember as I boarded the plane to Okinawa thinking about what it was going to be like walking off the plane on my return from Vietnam. There she would be standing there waiting for me and we would never be apart again. I tried not to think about it anymore. I was going to have a stop over at the Hawaiian Islands for four hours and I wanted to figure out what I could do in that short length of time. I wanted to make the most out of it. I found out when I got there we couldn't leave the airport. Most of my trip to Hawaii was standing in front of the loading zone looking at the scenery from afar. I hope to return someday for a visit.

My next stop would be Okinawa where it was so hot and humid I could barely stand it. The rest of my Recon training was the most difficult thing I had ever gone through. There were times I wanted to say fuck this shit and go to regular Marine Corps unit, but the Marine instructors were such bastards that it made me even more determined to make it. I realized later that it was their job to make or break us. My hardest training came during the concentration camp exercise. They used brain washing tactics to turn you against the United States and what it stood for. The training was to help in case you were captured by the enemy. We were given rice and water once a day. We were only allowed four hours of sleep per day. Believe me after a while you don't know if you are coming or going. I can only imagine what a real concentration camp would be like. My training as well as nineteen other guys was cut short due to the fact that they needed Recon Marines. They moved all of us over to indoctrination. There was a bad need for Recon personnel and they needed us now. Oh lucky me. I had to go for communications, just what they needed the most. I found out later that the life expectancy of a radioman was about six months.

CHAPTER 5

ARRIVAL IN VIETNAM

During the indoctrination training we were told that we would be flying in to Da Nang and that there would be soldiers leaving to go home. We were told not to look them in the eyes. They never said why, but I would soon learn. I landed in Da Nang June1966 the day before my eighteenth birthday. I had to report to Battalion Headquarters to be assigned to a unit. To get there I had to pass the embarking area for the troops that were going home. I will never forget the look on their faces. We were told not to look but how could I help it. They looked old and worn out. Their eyes were dead, dark and hollowed out. I wondered if I would end up like that someday. That same day I was assigned to the 1st Marine Division 9th regiment Hotel Company. There was nine Recon Marines being assigned to each company. One squad leader, four riflemen, two automatic riflemen, one sniper and one radioman, guess who that was. The 9th was at Phu Bai so I was transported there within an hour of receiving my orders. The things I would see, hear and feel from now on would change me for the rest of my entire life.

After arriving at Phu Bai I was assigned to a tent that held about fifteen Marines. The tent was empty because most of them were still out in the bush from the night before on an ambush. The next morning I couldn't believe what I saw. A truck pulled in and in it were about eight Marines. They had bandoleers on filled with bullets.

They had beards and mustaches; they looked like a bunch of Mexican bandits. They had a look in their eyes like I had never seen before. The same look that I would have before long. No one talked to me for about six hours. Finally the squad leader whose rank was a Corporal came to see me and said. First thing, keep your fucking mouth shut unless I ask you a question. You're going to carry this fucking PRC 25 radio. You're going to be my recon radioman. Do you have a fucking problem with that? If you do, then tell it to your cock. I don't want to hear it. I didn't say a word in fear that he would eat my face off right on the spot. I took the radio and set it down beside me. The PRC 25 radio was part of my recon training and I had always expected that was what my job was going to be as soon as I hit the bush. I just didn't expect to have it shoved up my ass. Again the only thing that really bothered me was that recon radioman only lasted about six months in the bush before they got their ass blown away. I did get up enough nerve to ask if the guy that had it before me was going home. All he said was yes, in a body bag. After he left I looked at the radio and saw the blood on the outside cover of the pack it was in. That's when I realized that I was really fucked. I was never going to see the real world again. I saw myself tore into a million pieces and or so fucked up that even my own Mother wouldn't be able to recognize me. His name was Williams and even though he was only a Corporal everyone called him Sergeant Rock behind his back. Just like in the comic books. That was because he was always a hard ass. It wasn't long before Cpl.Williams came back in and said saddle up we have a mission.

The first time I was dropped in a clearing by a chopper was on my first operation in Nam. I started walking towards the jungle and there was an air of reality, I was really in a war zone and there were people out there who would like to kill me. For a while it just didn't seem real, I still felt like I was in training, but it didn't take very long to forget about home. After a couple of weeks Vietnam would be my reality and the United States was just some place that I had heard about on the news. The jungle would become my only world. What I carried with me was my home and what was happening here was the only news that I cared about. I would hear the news about what was happening in United States, but none of it seemed to matter, it all seemed so trivial. Who cared about a store sale, a wage rise, a new model car, or someone being arrested. None of this was important. My reality was this jungle where the rules and laws of United States didn't exist anymore. This would be my real world from now on.

The ride up North was fairly uneventful. We were being choppered in close to the DMZ to a place called Dong Hoi. I don't think I gave much thought about what I might be getting into. It wasn't until I got out of the Chinook and on the dry, dusty ground that I suddenly realized that I was in a war zone. Here I was, a naïve, now eighteen year old kid, never been in a fight, never been in any trouble. I was in a foreign country and was expected to kill people who I have never seen before and who have never done me any wrong. We were shown where our company lines and tents were. We slept six to a tent, these tents had been there ever since the Task Force was built several years earlier and it looked (and smelled) like they still had the original cots in them.

After a couple of days` at my new home I was told to saddle up to go out on my first recon patrol, in the jungles of Vietnam. All the training I had didn't prepare me for the real thing. I took what they had told me to take, my forty-five cal hand gun, ammunition, a couple of grenades, and of course a box of C rations. This would be my first operation in the jungle. Again we were taken by chopper. I had never been on one before that had none of the safety conditions that it had during my training, such as shutting the doors or using seat belts. To this day I can still remember being crammed into the helicopter along with nine others with packs and weapons, trying to squeeze onto seats designed for people half our size. Then taking off, looking out through the open doorway at the tree tops flashing past not very far below us. Wondering who or what could be lurking in the dense jungle below. Not able to hear anything above the noise of the wind and the rotor blades. The chopper shaking so violently that it felt like it would fall to pieces. The door gunners holding on to their M60's. Then seeing the clearing, the pilot going in fast, a quick bumpy landing and then jumping out with what feels like the weight of another person on your back. Sliding a round in the chamber and quickly heading for the dark gloomy jungle.

The first couple of hours were a shock to the system. There were virtually no wild animals here as they had all been killed with the constant fighting. The jungle was very dense, hot, humid and quiet. All we could do was follow the person in front and make sure the person behind was still there. Sometimes the jungle was so dense that we'd only travel a few hundred meters and have to stop. Most of the time it was simply walk a few steps, then wait a couple of minutes, listen, then walk a few more steps, then listen again, and so on, and very rarely did we know what we were doing. Very little of the training I had applied here. We were all individuals and also part of a group in a huge jungle so dense that we didn't know where anyone else was, except the ones directly in front and behind.

Chapter 6

Night of the Ambush

In the late afternoon we stopped at a village to wait for night fall. We were going out under the cover of darkness to set up for an ambush. This was my first experience with marijuana. I was standing next to a hut when I heard one of three guys ask me if I wanted a toke. I had no idea what the hell he was talking about, so I asked him what's a toke? He held out his hand with something that looked like a cigarette. I told him I didn't smoke. He said maybe not now, but you will. He went back to smoking whatever it was. I walked away a few feet from them. I stood by another Marine who was watching them. I heard them talk about how good they were feeling and what beautiful colors they were seeing in a mud puddle that they were looking down at. I ask what is that their smoking and he said pot. Pot! What's pot? He said it's marijuana. I guess he could tell by the stupid look on my face that I still didn't understand. He said its pot, marijuana, Mary Jane. Where the hell did you come from the moon? Believe it or not I had never heard of marijuana before. I asked him if he smoked it and he said hell no. I'm not fucking up my brain with drugs. He then told me that I should just stay away from anything like that. At the time I didn't smoke, drink and I was still a virgin so it wasn't likely I was ever going to try it. I was a good Catholic boy. To this day I have never tried drugs, however; I now smoke cigarettes, drink vodka and I don't think I'm still a virgin.

When night fell it was time to go. We received our orders from Cpl. Williams. He had been in country for about four months on his second tour. He told me to stay close by him. I thought he wanted me to do that so that he would be able to have me call head quarters. It wasn't long before I really found out why. We had only gone for a short distance when an illumination round went off lighting up the sky almost like day light. We all hit the ground. While I was on the ground I moved just slightly, but that was all it took. When the round burned out and everything went dark again we got up and started out again. When the next round went up about two minutes later we hit the ground again. As I was going down on the ground I heard a couple of foot steps coming up fast behind me. Williams jumped on top of me and whispered in my ear that if I moved at all he would cut my throat with his K-bar. Believe me I didn't move a muscle. That was the last time he had to tell me not to move. When we arrived at the location where we were going to set up our ambush he said I would have the first watch. We set up in two's along the perimeter of our position with a M60 machine gun evenly spaced between us. Then it was a matter of clearing the ground for a space to sleep, eating some C rations and looking for bugs and or spiders. Everyone had to take their turn on watch through the night. About five minutes before total darkness everything was packed up and we "stood to", as this was the most likely time for an attack. Then it was straight to sleep, broken by a couple of hours on watch. We slept where we were positioned. Sometimes it was on ant nest, rocks, mud or whatever happened to be there. It was a matter of smoothing the ground as much as possible, laying down a ground sheet and in the wet trying to put up a "hootchie" (this was a waterproof sheet that was used as a sort of roof/tent). We were supposed to keep our boots on all night incase of an attack, but I got used to not ever taking mine off for days. I was damned if my toes were going to get eaten away by some scabby fungus or foot rot, which happened anyway. My radio pack was packed ready to go and I used it as a pillow. I placed my 45 cal next to me so that I could grab it in a hurry if needed. When it was your turn for watch the person waking you up did it very quietly and carefully, no one wants to get shaken roughly when you're asleep in a war zone. It was usually so dark that it was a matter of crawling along and feeling until you came to the guy who had the next watch. This was what it was like my first night and from then on. Every night we all took turns for two hours at a time. Sitting not talking, just listening, trying to see in the pitch black and looking forward to going back to sleep. At night when on guard if you heard a noise you fired first and asked questions later. No friendly forces moved around in the jungle at night, simply because you couldn't see squat', so if there was a noise you fired. Quite often (sometimes too often) someone would hear a noise and start blasting away. This would result in everyone else getting woken up with a heart rate of about a million beats a minute and a bucket load of adrenalin pumping through your veins, you'd grab your weapon, face outwards looking into a pitch black jungle and lie there quietly listening. If you heard a noise to your front you had to decide whether to fire or not, if you fired and there was someone there then they'd see the flash from your rifle and could have shot back and there may have been more of them than you. This type of incident happened to all of us regularly, as there were always strange noises at night. Especially, when you're sitting in a jungle at night where the imagination and fear become very real.

After we were in position for the night (my first night in the jungle) Cpl. Williams tapped me on the shoulder and said you have the first watch. I sat there while everyone laid down to get a little sleep. It had only been a few minutes when Williams put his hand around my mouth and his K-bar on my throat. He said if you fall asleep you will never wake up. I'll cut your throat and leave you here. I was so scared of him by now that I believed everything he said. Looking back now I understand what he was trying to do. Keep me alive. I sometimes wonder if he really would have done it. I was on watch for about an hour and ten minutes when I heard something. I didn't open up with my 45 caliber, instead I reached over and tapped the guy next to me on the shoulder while putting my hand close to his face, just incase he said something loud. Noise carries in the night for a long ways. All of a sudden Cpl. Williams opened fire along with a couple of other Marines. We had caught a squad size patrol in our ambush. They returned fire on us. I can still remember thinking my God, is this going to happen every night and is this for real. I opened up with my weapon. I don't think I hit anything that night. I wasn't sure how I was going to feel about killing a human. Later on I would know the feeling and would have to work through it. The longer I was in Nam the easier it became. I even started to put notches in the handle of my 45, just like they did in the western movies. What a dumb shit I was. The fire fight lasted only for about three minutes but it seemed an eternity.

I heard screaming. It was coming from one of our guys. Cpl Williams put his hand over the wounded mans mouth and said, take the pain. Take the pain! You got to be kidding. I was on the radio calling for a medivac and trying to find out where the pick up point would be. One of the Marines turned on his flash light to see where the guy had been hit. It was in his back close to his spine. There was a big hole and blood and steam was coming out of it. I had never seen anything like that before and I said, what is that! The guy holding the flash light said hell that's **White Hot and Red**. He had been hit with an AK 47 bullet. It was a tracer round. A tracer round burns hotter than the other rounds in a magazine. Every fifth bullet in a magazine is a tracer round so that at night you can see them to direct you're fire. The steam was from his flesh burning. I'll never forget that first fire fight or that bullet wound. Although I would go on to see worse wounds and be in worse fire fights. I got the medivac pick up point; it was about a half mile away where there was a clearing for a chopper to land. We had to take turns carrying the wounded man and his gear. After he was medivaced we sat up another ambush until morning.

CHAPTER 7

THE NEXT MORNING

When morning came Cpl. Williams came over to me and said you did fine. Then he asked me how I felt about my first fire fight. I told him I was scared. He then said something that I never expected. He said, so was I. That's all he said and walked away. I guess everyone gets scared, unless you're some kind of a super hero. We made our way back to the pick up point to board the chopper. We were taken back to Dong Hoi behind company lines. We got some chow and some of the other guys got some more sleep. I wrote about what happened in my diary.

The next recon patrol would take place about two days later. This time it was a ten mile recon patrol. It would be five miles out the first day and hold up in a village until night fall to set up another ambush. Then it would be five miles the next day, back to company lines. Jungle warfare isn't like in the movies where the fearless jungle fighters hack their way through the jungle with machetes on well worn paths. The first person (the forward rifle-men) had to make his own path using a pair of loppers, quietly cutting one branch at a time while keeping his eyes open for any VC and the only thing that the rest of us could do was to follow along. It was always hot and humid or wet and freezing. We rarely spoke and when we did it was always in a quiet whisper. One of the greatest pleasures was when we'd halt for several minutes on recon patrol and we could get a few minutes rest by sitting on the ground just to take the weight of the pack off our shoulders.

If you've ever watched any jungle war movies and all of a sudden the bad guys shoot at the good guys and then the good guys dive into the jungle and right away they know where to shoot at the bad guys. Well it's not quite like that. The jungle was so dense that most times it was only possible to see a person a few meters in front and behind you. If shots were fired you wouldn't know where they came from and while lying on the ground in a tropical jungle you can't see anything. You certainly don't stick your head up and look around to see who's shooting at you. If someone is dressed in dark colors and is standing still in a tropical jungle you can pass within a few meters and not even see them. This wasn't a war where there was a "front line" the North Vietnamese Regular Army consisted of very professional and skillful soldiers and was a force to be reckoned with. Where as the Viet Cong (VC) could be anyone. Young women and boys that were extremely hard to find. They could be the person you talk to during the day and then the same one you shoot at in the jungle. The end result of this was that most of us simply followed the person in front through the jungle while who ever was forward scout would quietly lead the way with safety catch off and eyes and ears wide open. For me this was a war of walk, stop, listen, walk, stop, listen.

Despite the difficulties and hardships of living in an inhospitable jungle we all got along very well with each other. Our world was our small group of eight to ten guys at a time. We lived together and relied totally on each other, especially the person you "slept" with at night. His name was Benny. The two of you were alone in a black noiseless jungle. Probably one of the worst things about the jungle was the bugs. In the dry season there were red tree ants (weaver ants) that made nests in trees and if you brushed against them you would be instantly covered with hundreds of biting ants, there were ticks which caused a painful red lump, but were more of a nuisance than anything else. There were scorpions, large (jumper) ants, termite nests, spiders, centipedes and snakes. Then in the winter there were leeches and even mud crabs. What a nice vacation spot. The humidity and heat was so high that wearing clothes for more than a few months caused the cloth to simply rot and fall apart. I usually carried two pairs of socks that I rarely washed. I just turned them inside out, swapped from my left foot to my right foot and so on.

The Boots were another thing, they were the greatest. The leather would get hard dried and cracked very quickly, but they held up. I soon found out that you don't wear underwear in a jungle, rashes were easy to come by and hard to get rid of. Clothes were worn loose and comfortable. In a jungle looks aren't important, but comfort is. I smelled terrible, but as we all smelled the same, it wasn't noticeable. We didn't carry any identification except for "dog tags"; I destroyed any addresses and identifying information on any letters that I had (if you lost it and the VC got it they could write to who ever sent you the letter.)

The training I had didn't really prepare me for what I would need to take in the jungle. I very quickly found out that mosquito repellent is useless, as were waterproof ponchos, air mattresses and about half the food in the ration packs. You may have figured out from this that the

Hollywood image of the really cool looking Rambo killer, silently darting through the jungle in his designer military gear, carrying a rifle, a knife and not much else may be a bit short of reality. We used to get a re-supply, usually by chopper before our rations ran out. This also included a change of clothes sometimes, a couple of boxes of C rations and any mail from home. I rarely got any and to this day I don't know why. If any of the rations from the packs that I got had holes in them I got rid of them. Water was the biggest problem especially in the dry heat of a Vietnam summer. I always carried sterilizing tablets because; I all too often would have to use river or rice paddy water.

The food in the ration packs was surprisingly good. The packs were made to sustain us. Not to be enjoyed. However, the packs had small containers of peaches or pound cake, so you could make up a meal. A lot of the stuff in the ration packs are similar to some of the kid's snacks that are sold in the supermarkets today, jam, marmalade, small packs of cracker biscuits with cheese spread, small tins of fruit or cake.

Chapter 8

Sniper in the Village

The five mile recon patrol went well, but I was glad when we reached the village. Five miles is a long way when you're humping a radio, water and rations through the jungle. When we were close to the village we sent in a couple of Marines to check it out. All too often the village might be full of NVA soldiers confiscating rice and hiding weapons along with ammunitions to come back for later. Also they would recruit the young men of the village. If they refused they would shoot them. A lot of villages were tore to pieces and set on fire by the NVA. I will admit that the American solders were not much better at times. When the two Marines returned from their recognizance they said everything looked ok. Cpl.Williams said lets get going ladies. He loved calling us that. On the way in to the village we took a couple of rounds from a sniper. Everyone hit the dirt. I couldn't believe it, here we go again. Another round was fired and hit close to me, probably because I was carrying the radio. Everyone started firing in the direction of the tree line where the shots had come from. When all the shooting stopped a couple of guys made their way to the tree line, but found nothing. Cpl.Williams was pissed off because he thought the villagers knew there was a sniper in the tree line. He had us check all the huts to see if there were any false floors where there might be hidden weapons. We didn't find anything, but Cpl.Williams still carried on with the villagers as if they were hiding something. He slapped some of them around and was waving his rifle around like he was going to shoot them. I didn't know what to think. I just wanted to be somewhere else, like home. He decided that we would stay outside the village until night fall to make sure that the VC weren't informed where we were or what direction we went in to set up our ambush. That didn't make some of the other guys to happy. They wanted pussy. The young boys of the villages, about nine to ten years old, would sell their sisters that were around fifteen or sixteen years old for five or ten dollars. That doesn't sound like much money, but back then five dollars could buy allot, especially on the black market if it was American money. Besides there was always more than one guy so she could make fifteen to twenty dollars or should I say her brother. It was probably a good thing we didn't go into the village, I was still pretty new to this new world and I had heard the stories about how the villagers were sometimes really VC.

Your back would be sticky with sweat and your flak jacket would cling and chill your back. A bad odor flows upward out of the open neck of your utility shirt and you realize that bad smell is you. The Sun is pounding down on your helmet and your head bakes. The sweat pours down from your head and burns your eyes. It continues to flow along the edge of your nose down to your mouth and you can taste the salt. Your hot, tired and smell like dog shit. You need a drink. Next think you know you hear a young voice ask you if you want a drink of soda. You see a young girl with a smile on her face, you say yes. She pops a hole in the top of the can and pours it into a paper cup full of chipped ice. You drink it down in a large mouthful along with small chips of ice. Down your throat it goes along with the soda. By this time you realize, way too late, that slivers of glass are cutting your stomach from the inside out. The games they played in Vietnam were deadly. Like a truck coming down the road filled with Marines, they see a group of small boys that offer loaves of bread to the Marines riding on the back of the vehicle. The truck is also loaded with supplies. All of a sudden the truck heaves in the air and the Marines are thrown to the ground blown into pieces. The loaf of bread contained a hand grenade. I felt the more I could stay away from the villages the better.

Chapter 9

Benny

When night fell we moved out in single file to our location and sat up for the night. I had the first watch. It was a quiet night. Almost to quiet except for the bombing that was taking place far off in the distance. It was a B-52 dropping her load. This was the first time I had ever witnessed it. The ground was vibrating softly and the sky in the distance would light up, sort of like the Forth of July. It sort of made me sleepy. I spent some of my time on watch thinking about a big hamburger and a glass of milk. I thought about how great it would be to have one right then. I guess you just don't appreciate things until you can't have them. Nothing happened that night and I actually was able to sleep without waking up every ten minutes.

When morning came we ate some chow and then saddled up to make our way back to company lines. I just wanted to go back the way we came, but Cpl. Williams took a different route. At least the route back wasn't as bad as the route coming. The jungle wasn't as thick and we stopped to rest more often. There wouldn't be any new patrols for a week. The one good thing about being in recon was that you didn't have ambush patrols every night. There were other patrols that filled in. It was nice just to sit and get some rest. I spent some time writing in my diary and letters to Lana and my family. It was during this time I first met Benny. He had been in country one month longer than I had, assigned to the 5th Marines. He was transferred to my company because there was a need for a couple of recon riflemen. One of them was going home and the other one was the guy who got shot in the back a week or so ago. I guess he wasn't coming back. I liked Benny the first time I met him. He was Mexican or is it Spanish American these days. He asked me if it was alright if he took the cot next to mine and I said you bet. I'm glad we had a few minutes to talk because I was able to tell him about Cpl.Williams. I told him what happened to me the first time I met him. Just about then Cpl. Williams came in and told all of us to listen up. He told us he was being assigned to another Recon team somewhere to the Northwest of the DMZ. He said that's all I can tell you. Then he said all of you keep your ass wired tight and you just might make it out of here. Then he said, believe it or not, I think you're a great bunch of guys. I might see you back in the real world someday. He had another Marine with him that he introduced as our new squad leader Cpl Cain. His name was Tristan Cain Jr and he looked like he belonged on an advertising poster for the Marine Corps. He was six foot two, eyes of blue. I would bet that when he walked in a room in his dress blues that all the girls would fall over. Let's just say he was the ideal Marine. Enough of that or I'll start sounding weird.

CHAPTER 10

HANOI HANNAH

We would be in camp for the next week, so I really got to know Benny. We talked about everything. He grew up poor like I did and we both joined the Marines for the same reason. I guess that's why he became my best friend over there. We played cards and listened to Hanoi Hannah. Her name was Trinh Thi Ngo. We called her Hanoi Hannah. She called herself Hu Houng, "the fragrance of autumn". But her job was to chill and frighten us, not to charm and seduce. She would say, "How are you GI Joe. It seems to me that most of you are poorly informed about the war, to say nothing about a correct explanation of your presence over here. Nothing is more confused than to be ordered into a war to die or to be maimed for life without the faintest idea of what's going on. American GIs don't fight this unjust immoral and illegal war of Johnson's. Get out of Vietnam now and live. This is the voice of Vietnam Broadcasting from Hanoi, capitol of the Democratic republic of Vietnam. Our program for American GIs can be heard at 1630 hours. Now here's Connie Francis singing "who's sorry now."

In Vietnam you tuned into whatever newscasts your transistor radio would pick up. It was reassuring to know that you were missing that big offensive somewhere in the next Province and that you could spend another few days in the so called rear. BBC was the first choice for radio news and was the most reliable, but often hard to pick up. On US Armed Forces Radio even a major battle could sound like a minor skirmish if it didn't favor US or ARVN forces, but you learned to read between the lines of their newscasts. Sometimes you would hear your own TV or radio reports from State side broadcasts, picked up and rebroadcast over US Armed Forces Radio. As long as they didn't mention American set backs or were critical of Washington policy.

Radio Hanoi could be heard in most areas of North Vietnam, particularly at night and I would listen to her just for a few laughs. The soldier's radio was, after his rifle, his most valued possession. Like his rifle, the radio was usually wrapped in frayed black tape for protection. Marines would laugh and make jokes over Hannah's attempts to scare us into going home or her suggestions to frag an officer. If our unit was mentioned, a great cheer went up. Mine was mentioned allot. Even though I acted like it didn't bother me, it did. We would ask each other how the hell she could know what she did, the stories and her insights. Her military intelligence grew with each broadcast and she was often credited with broadcasting Viet Cong offensives in advance and within hours of a battle knowing the names and home towns of dead American Marines. She would even sometimes tell us when we were going to be hit with 82mm mortar rounds. The war time words of Hanoi Hannah were part of the loud sound track for the Vietnam War. It may have been the first war fought to rock n 'roll. For me and a lot of other Marines the beat came with a message. The winning side was in Hanoi and the misinformation side was the US in Saigon. Even so, radio brought music and messages with a familiar sound to me and Benny. We thought the war was at the end of the earth. To me it didn't matter who was broadcasting, Radio Hanoi or US Armed Forces Radio. After all I had been in Vietnam for over two months. It seemed like a life time.

Chapter 11

The Morgue

Word came down that we were being transferred to the 2nd Bn 26th Marines. They needed a recon team in the Phong Dien area. We were going to be choppered in about an hour, so there wasn't much time to write letters or even get something to eat. We boarded the chopper and we were on our way. When we got there we were met by a Staff Sergeant Henry. He showed us where to drop our gear. The next two months proved to be very active. The first few weeks were spent on the final phase of Operation Apache. We were to run recon missions by day. We would sweep the area for booby traps and punji pits. At night we would go back out to assure that the North Vietiness Army (NVA) wasn't trying to move back into Phong Dien Song. The NVA moved under the cover of darkness most of the time.

It was during this time that we were heavily engaged at close range with the NVA. They were pounding us with mortar attacks every two hours and we were taking on heavy casualties. One week later the Battalion would be in almost constant contact with the NVA. We were now being subjected to heavy SA, Mortar, Rocket, and Artillery fire. Air power was called in but really didn't seem to do any good. My recon team was assigned to go on patrol with the 1st platoon. We now had forty-six men which was a far cry from six of us. I guess I felt a little bit safer. This would be the first time I was wounded. We were out about five hundred meters from the perimeter. I was filling in for the Platoon radioman and I was with Lieutenant Landers who wanted to be at the front of the platoon. We were about fifty feet from the point man whose name was Pfc. Leon Johnson. The point man is supposed to make sure we didn't walk into an ambush. Well the last thing Leon saw was a bullet to his forehead. We had walked right into the middle of a platoon size ambush and they opened up on us with AK 47's and machine guns.

I was hit in the right leg with a tracer round from a machine gun. The bullet went into the back of my leg and came out the front. At first I didn't even know I was hit. My leg jerked a little, but when I looked down I saw the blood pouring down my leg. Lucky for me it was a white hot tracer round because it burned the bullet hole partly shut. I hit the ground just as Lt. Landers took ten hits in the chest. He was dead before he hit the ground. I called into the CP (command post) and advised what was happening. Then I called for medivac. SSgt Henry took over the Platoon and started directing fire to the NVA. He asked me if I was ok and put a battle dressing on my leg. I was fine from what I could tell, but I couldn't believe I was really hit and that they were trying to kill me. I was down behind a small bush returning fire with my 45 cal, but I really couldn't see much. SSgt Henry took my radio transmitter and called in artillery. Cpl Lee who was one of the squad leaders came running over to report to Sgt Henry but never made it. He took rounds in his lower stomach. A couple of other Marines grabbed him up and brought him over to us. William Harris (Billy) the Navy corpsman was one of the guy's. I can still remember to this day what happened next. One of Cpl Lee's bullet wounds was pouring blood and Billy couldn't dress all the wounds at one time. So he took my hand and shoved my index finger in one of the worst bullet holes. He said don't move your finger until I tell you to. Cpl Lee looked and sounded like he was dying. He kept asking for his Mom. That really got to me. I would go on to hear that phrase again and again from dieing Marines. I wondered if it was like that in all wars. Mothers raise a son and the Government sends them off to war, unless of course you parents are rich or a big shot in the Government.

The artillery rounds were starting to come in now and the fire fight was over. The NVA took off in a hell of a hurry. The first medivac chopper arrived so we started putting wounded men on it. Then another two arrived. That's when I realized that there were a lot of wounded. SSgt Henry told me to hop on the last chopper so I gave him my radio. When we got to the rear I hopped off and said take that guy and that one I'm fine. My leg was still bleeding and it hurt like hell but at least I could walk and some of these guys were really fucked up. They cut away the skin that was around the bullet hole and sewed it shut. Gave me a shot in the leg, dressed and bandaged the wound and told me to come back the next day. I reported to the CP and asked them what I was supposed to do. They told me to wait right there, they needed me to go over to the morgue to identify some of the dead Marines from the ambush. While I was standing there Chino walked up to me and asked what the hell happened. He just got back from R&R.and was told he would have to go with me to identify the dead. I liked Chino, he was a real cool guy and even though he wasn't in recon Benny and I hung around him, playing cards and talking about what we were going to do when we all got back to the real world.

Chino and I reported to the morgue and when we walked in I couldn't believe my eyes. There was this guy sitting on a stool going through body parts that were on the floor. He was tossing them on to ponchos. Another guy who was shaved headed and very tall, walked in from a side door. His arms looked like they were so long that his knuckles were dragging on the floor. He came up to us and asked what we wanted. Chino told him why we were both there. Chino just got through telling him when the guy on the stool turned to us, held up a bloody foot and asked us if we wanted a piece of leg. Then he tossed the foot onto one of the ponchos. It looked like there was about nine or ten ponchos laying around with arms, legs, hands and fingers on them. I didn't see any heads. Finally this knuckle dragger said come in here. It was the refrigerator. He opened the door and started calling for a couple of the dead guys by name. Chino and I just looked at each other. He would call out Johnson! Oh Johnson where are you. When he found who he was looking for he said, there you are! Then he would pull out the tray, opened the body bag and have both of us identified them, one by one until we were through. By this time I was really getting freaked out. Finally we were done and told to stand by the door out of the way because a chopper had just landed and they were bringing in more dead from a different battle. While I was standing there I heard a clinking sound from the back of me. When I turned around I looked down right into the face of a head that had been severed from the torso of a body. His head was lying on his back and one of his severed arms was lying next to his severed legs. He was the most fucked up person I had ever seen. I must have gone into semi shock because I started laughing. I laughed and laughed while tears started pouring down my face. Chino looked at me and said, man you are fucked up. He was bothered by what he was seeing also, but had already seen things like this before. He poured some water over my head and I started to come out of it. I told him I was sorry and he said don't worry about it. It hit me hard the first time I saw something like that too. We made our way back to the tent and I sat down on one of the cots. I just couldn't get what I had seen out of my head.

Chapter 12

Dear John

Chino went to see if there was any mail for him. There was always mail for Chino. He came from a large family and they were all very close. So he got letters every week. Sometimes you could go for weeks before the Marines could get the mail to you, so Chino would get about ten letters at a time. I was lucky to get two letters a month. Just as I was going to get up and go see if I had any mail, Chino came in and said, hey a couple of letters for you. One was from my good buddy Duane back home. That letter would have to wait because the other one was from Lana. I couldn't wait to open it and read how she loved and missed me. Her letter came at the right time, I really needed it. Well the letter didn't start out Dear John, it had my name on it, but that's what it was, a fucking Dear John letter. She had met some guy in the Navy reserve stationed at Sand Point in Seattle. She went on to tell me how waiting for me was just too hard on her, worrying about me getting hurt or killed. Her Mother was right. She knew that her daughter wouldn't wait for me or anyone else. I thought to myself, you stupid bitch. Chino could see that I was really upset and asked me what was wrong. I handed him the letter. I couldn't even finish reading it. After he read it he said, fuck her. He said you know of course only a WOMAN would send a Dear John letter, to a guy in a war zone. Their all the same, their all bitches. Do you really want a girl friend like this? You know you're not the first guy to get one of these and you're certainly not going to be the last. You need to just forget about her and don't let it mess with your head. Not over here or you're a dead. Someday you're going home and then you can tell the bitch to get fucked, I'm too good for you.

He was right, I already knew a couple of guys who had gotten Dear John letters. One of the guys was married. I just wanted to get home now in one piece. To this day I still don't really like women or trust them. I guess that's why I never tell them how I feel or what I'm thinking. It's safer that way. Chino said hey! You know what? There's a movie in the field tonight and I got a bottle of Silver Fox whiskey. We spent the next two hours talking about how women were the lowest creatures on earth. I didn't drink so Chino said let me show you how to do it. Take a shot of whiskey and then chase it with a shot of Coca-Cola. Well after a few shots I started feeling light headed, but great. We started out to go to the field where the movie was going to be, but I didn't get very far before the bandage on my leg started falling down around my ankle. The wound in my leg was starting to bleed and the blood ran down my leg. I kept trying to pull the bandage back up where it belonged, but it just fell down again. Finally I just hung on to it. The movie was just getting started and I was standing there watching. That's the last thing I remember. The next morning I woke up with a screaming headache and sicker than a dog. It was just getting light outside. The bandage was down around my ankle again and there was blood all over me and the cot. I got sick and threw up. I drank some water and went back to sleep. Later in the morning Chino woke me up and said don't forget your suppose to go to have your bandage check out. He laughed about what had happened the night before. He said you were standing there and then you fell flat on your face. I helped you up and carried you back here. I didn't know you were a virgin to whiskey. I washed my face and I started feeling a little better. Later that morning I had my wound checked out and was told that it would be a couple of days more before I could return to duty. Chino was being shipped out right away and said I'll see you when you get back. I told him to say hi to Benny for me. He said don't worry I got a story to tell him now. I said thanks allot good buddy. I went back to the tent to read the letter from Duane. He had gotten drafted into the army. He was just finishing up his basic training.

Chapter 13

Hill of the Angels

The next two days went by fast and it was time to be shipped back to my unit. My leg still hadn't healed and was still bleeding a little, but that really didn't matter to the Marines. What's a little bullet wound. When I got back to my unit nothing had changed. I was happy to see Benny again. Our unit was still being hit daily by heavy SA, Mortar, Rocket and Artillery fire. Also my recon unit started pulling recon missions every other day. There were small fire fights here and there and we lost a few marines, but for the most part the area was starting to become more and more secure. This condition continued until the end of Aug 1966. By then the NVA was on the move to some other unknown location.

On Sept 10th my recon unit was reassigned to the 1st Marine Division 9th regiment Echo Company. They were at a hell hole called Con Thien. Echo Company along with three other companies had the great duty assignment of trying to protect the outpost from being over run again by the NVA. The outpost was being used as a forward position. Con Thien was a hill 158 meters high. It was actually a cluster of three small hills. It was an ugly bare patch of red mud. Local missionaries called it "The Hill of The Angels" due to the massive amount of casualties attributed to the hill. The hills were only large enough to accommodate a reinforced battalion. It was the Northwest anchor of what we Marines called the "McNamara Line."

The "McNamara Line" was actually a 600-meter clearing constructed by the 11th Engineers as a buffer zone from the Laotian border to the South China Sea. The "Strip" was originally constructed for the placement of sensors to detect any enemy troop movements, but the project was called off in favor of fortifying Khe Sahn that was still under construction.

Con Thien was clearly visible from 9th Marine Headquarters at Dong Ha to the South. We could also see Gio Linh a "Firebase" Northeast of Con Thien. We knew that if the NVA over ran Con Thien and Gio Linh they would have a clear path to the South. It was our job not to let this happen. We would run patrols and ambushes every day to keep the NVA on the move. We wanted to make certain they couldn't build fixed positions in and around the area. It was a hard job. We would destroy a bunker complex one day and a couple of days later it would be rebuilt. We actually found bunkers as close as 1000 meters from Con Thien. There was not much we could do about the NVA in the area. We were short handed and had such a large area to patrol that the NVA could move around freely without much chance of detection. We would patrol an area and they would return as soon as we were gone.

We had a couple of nicknames for Con Thien. We called it "Our Turn in the Barrel" or "The Meat grinder." Almost daily we would receive at least 200 rounds of NVA incoming. I really don't remember a day in which we didn't get hit with incoming rounds of some sort. We also suffered something that was almost unheard of elsewhere in South Vietnam. It was called "shell shock" and it was not unusual. The constant pounding every day could make you go Nuts. You would sit there on edge, wondering if the next round that came in would have your name on it. In official Marine Corps history they make mention of the "Die Marker" bunkers. They were supposed to be well reinforced with timbers and steel. My unit had some but Benny and I never got to try any of those. We were in holes in the Mud!

Echo Company 2/9 was on one of the small hills on the Southern edge of Con Thien right next to the LZ and the (I guess what you would call the main gate.) We had hardly any protection at all. Echo Company caught more than their share of incoming because; every time a chopper or a truck arrived they would shell the shit out of us. In the month of September from the 19th to the 27th, we received over 3,000 rounds of incoming. I will never forget September 1966. I thought the NVA was going to blow Con Thien off the map with artillery, rockets and mortars. We took over 1200 rounds on a single day. I don't think there was hardly a spot on that hill not hit by an incoming round of some sort. To that point and time in the war this was the most incoming rounds ever taken by a unit in Vietnam in one day. That's a lot of incoming rounds for such a small place. There was almost no place to hide.

Every time a chopper would arrive, incoming rounds would follow. That made it very hard for us to be re-supplied. During one week in September a chopper didn't touch down at Con Thien except for a Medivac. They would just drop the boxes of chow and mail out the doors without landing. The Marine Corps thought the choppers were too valuable to lose. We had to ration food and water sometimes going three days without food and two days without water. Trying to eat after three days without food made your teeth bleed and your mouth sting like it was burning.

Every night the NVA would probe our lines to try and find a weakness they could penetrate and of course there were always the fucking NVA snipers. This was also the time one of the guys I knew had a rocket hit right next to his hole. I remember him staggering out of his hole with blood running out of both ears and his mouth. I never saw him again after that day. We medivac'd him out of there. He was going home. I was glad he was going home, but I wished it were me. I remember rounds hitting all around us that day. I believed God was watching over me and Benny. It was really hard on the "Brain Bucket" (your head) just sitting there waiting for the next barrage, the one that could take your life. The stress of the constant incoming artillery barrages could drive you insane. It would have been different if we could have shot back at them. Then we would have been able to get a little relief.

As if this wasn't bad enough already, we also had to put up with the Monsoon rains. Our holes would fill with water and we would have to bail them out four or five times a day. Some of the guys had "immersion foot" and their feet would bleed and hurt like hell. Then there was the damn mud. You walked in it, you sat in it, you slept in it and you even ate it. There was just no escaping it. Because the choppers not being able to land due to incoming rounds. Not only did we run out of C-rations, but that also meant no toilet paper. So we started to tear strips of cloth from the bottoms of our trousers to wipe our butts. At one period we were not re-supplied for over three days. During that time we actually scrounged around in our trash pits trying to find something to eat. The choppers kept flying over us trying to re-supply other units. At least the choppers came to pick up our wounded. One of the door gunners on a chopper that finally brought us food saw the look in our eyes and decided he better drop the food out that door. We knew the pilots were only following orders, but that didn't change the fact that we were hungry and we were pissed off. There's nothing in the world crazier than a marine hungry and angry with a loaded weapon in his hand.

Chapter 14

The Corpsman

We stayed glued to our holes for most of the day. One morning a rocket came screaming in and hit about ten yards behind my hole, it was a dud Rocket round that didn't go off. It was so eerie. Finally one guy got up enough nerve to get out of his hole and went up to investigate it. It was green and about eight feet long. It had funny looking Russian writing on it. It really pissed me off. Not only did we have the NVA and the Chinese fighting against us, now the Russians were fighting us too. The engineers sat a charge and blew the rocket up. It wasn't before long due to the dirt in the water that I got the shits (dysentery) and decided to take a chance and go out in front of my hole and dig a "Cat hole" and take a crap. Just as I was finishing up I heard the sound of rockets taking off in the distance. I heard Benny yelling "Incoming." I was already halfway up the hill by then. I hadn't had time to fasten my pants so my ass was hanging out. I was holding them up with my hand and attempting to run the rest of the way up the hill to my hole, but it was muddy and I slipped and fell. I scrambled the rest of the way to my hole on my hands and knees with my pants down to my ankles. I fell into my hole. The second my body hit the mud in the bottom of my hole, a rocket round hit. Then another that threw mud all over us. The concussion made my ears ring and for awhile I couldn't hear anything.

When morning came the incoming had stopped and I tried to get out of my hole, but I couldn't. I was stuck in a foot of mud in the bottom of my hole. I had to get Benny to help me out. When he finally got me out of my hole he laughed about how funny I looked trying to run for cover with my butt hanging out. When I looked at him I started laughing too. It felt good to laugh. There wasn't much laughing going on at Con Thien during the month of late September early October. We had ponchos covering the top of our holes that we were using for shelter from the rain. They were a little shredded from the Rocket blast. I think if I hadn't hit my hole when I did I would have looked just like our ponchos. Swiss cheese!

Even though we were receiving incoming rounds it didn't mean that patrols stopped going out. I remember a patrol trying to go out of our perimeter right in front of my hole. We started to take incoming rounds again and the Marines in the patrol were jumping into the closest holes to them. My hole was close and five Marines piled in on top of me. That was great, it was the most protection that I had in a long time. I still remember thinking that my hole couldn't have been capable of holding that many Marines, but it did! In came another Rocket barrage that caused allot of damage.

The CP bunker (command post) was about thirty-five yards off to my right and up the hill about twenty-five yards. The CP took a direct hit by a rocket round. There were two Marines in the bunker. The LT (Lieutenant) and his company radioman. There was a scream for help and the Corpsman ran to the bunker. There were at least two screams for help before the Corpsman got there. I came up out of my hole and so did Benny. I saw the Corpsman, from now on I'll call him Doc, come up and out of his hole and sprinting across the top of the hill and down to the CP bunker, during which time he was totally exposed to enemy fire. The rounds were hitting all around him and it's a miracle that he wasn't hit himself. He ran the forty yards in no time at all and jumped into that bunker. The Lieutenant and radioman were badly hit. One of the Marines from our recon unit named Reed arrived at the bunker first and said that when he arrived the LT looked up at him and said thank God and then went into a coma. Reed tucked the LT's guts back into his stomach and was holding them in when Doc arrived. Doc immediately covered the gapping wound in the LT's stomach with a battle dressing and he worked on both of them to trying to stop the bleeding. Doc, Reed and some other Marines pulled them from the bunker to another hole. The radioman lost a leg but he made it. I never heard what happened to the LT.

The entire time that Doc was there everyone was screaming at him and Reed to get the hell out of the bunker. Lucky for them they did because another rocket came in and hit in the same place. I thought to myself how close they came to death. Benny and I started to look around and saw how close they came to hitting our Ammo Bunker!

"Holy Shit! Benny said. "That was close!"

Doc and Reed probably deserved a medal that day for their actions, but they got nothing. Hell, if our Corpsmen received all of the medals they deserved, they probably wouldn't be able to walk from the weight of them.

CHAPTER 15

SOUNDS OF THE NIGHT

The day after the barrage that bunker was torn down never to be used again, although it was stupid to tear the bunker down. The NVA undoubtedly had every bunker and hole on the hill charted. I think the NVA had a spotter in a tree line about 500 meters away. I remember lying at night trying to sleep, but sleep was impossible. I was far too nervous. All I could manage to do was close my eyes and hope to get some rest. I would lay there with my eyes closed and my feet dangling in my fox hole and I could hear every single sound in the area. I remember I could hear the Rocket rounds when they were taking off in the distance and I would try to be the first one in the hole. You could hear them taking off just cross the Ben Hai River in North Vietnam. We were that close! I can honestly say that I never got any real sleep the entire time I was at Con Thien. If you ever really went to sleep you might not wake up.

I remember our Artillery and Mortar crews doing a great job of trying to keep the NVA gunners off our backs. We hit them with everything we had. I heard some real big guns firing some days. I think I was told that Navy ships were firing support for us. They had huge guns. It must have been hell on the receiving end of those babies. I also remember being bounced around in my hole by the shock waves from B-52 Bombers dumping their loads of 1,000 lb. bombs. It was a sight to see watching the B-52s at work. There were large pieces of shrapnel flying in the air. Big twisted pieces of hot metal that would tear the skin right off the bones. You had to feel just a little sorry for them. Very little. Sometimes it was like watching a movie. I also saw a lot of Huey's go down after being hit by NVA SAMs (surface to air missiles.)

I remember one chopper to the north one day was being chased by a NVA SAM (Surface to Air Missile). I thought the chopper was crashing because it was coming down so fast. The chopper landed fast in a zigzag downward motion. Then this big slow SAM appeared with a flame coming out of the tail. All of a sudden out of nowhere came a US Phantom Jet doing a victory roll right over the top of our heads and the SAM slowly turned in pursuit of the jet. The jet was flying circles around it. Then the jet lead the missile out and far away from our perimeter and the missile exploded.

I believe that had we not had supporting arms at Con Thien we would have been over run many times over. The one thing about my stay at Con Thien that really sticks in my mind is a picture of a Marine sitting in a puddle of blood with battle dressings on. He was sitting on a poncho with both his legs blown off from the waist down. He was numb from morphine and in shock from loss of blood. He was smoking a cigarette very calmly as if nothing had even happened. He was waiting for a Medivac. He probably died in the chopper ride back.

When my recon team arrived at Con Thien we had ten men. When we left we only had four. Cpl Cain, Benny, Reed, and me. That's why Con Thien was called the "The Meat grinder!"

CHAPTER 16

HILL 881 NORTH AND SOUTH

By October we were re-assigned to the 3rd Marines 26th regiment India Company. India Company of the 3rd Battalion 26th Marines had just fought their way up to the top of Hill 881 South for the second time. Hill 881 South was a regimental outpost about four miles west of the Khe Sanh Combat Base (KSCB). The North Vietnamese Army (NVA) activity was small until October when a Marine recon team was ambushed near 881 North about two miles directly north of 881 South. Both hills had been sites of fierce battles earlier in the year when the 3rd Marine Regiment took heavy casualties seizing them. Hill 881 South had been taken back, but 881 North was abandoned because the shape of the hill and the hard terrain around it made it a very poor defensive position.

When an India Company sent in another recon team to recover gear abandoned by the first recon team they ran into a lot of NVA. We were brought in, all four of us, to support a recon force to Hill 881 North the following day. I believe it was Mike Company of the 3rd Battalion less one platoon that was sent to Hill 881 South to hold it while India Company made their way toward Hill 881 North. We along with India Company ran head on into a NVA battalion coming south. The siege of the Khe Sanh valley was beginning although it wouldn't be until my second tour in the first part of the year 1968 that the NVA would trap us at Camp Carroll Khe Sanh base.

The North Vietnamese had been ready and waiting. They were dug in deeply into an interconnected system of fighting bunkers, with as much as six feet of packed earth and logs overhead. They were camouflaged and aiming down from cut outs of the underbrush. The NVA troops had held their fire until our leading Marine units of about 60 men were only a few feet away. The initial volley of gun fire killed scores of young Marines and as the survivors scrambled for cover the fucking enemy marksman, firing rifles with telescopic sights, shot radio operators, and machine gunners through the head. I had bullets fly by my head, but I'm glad the sniper who shot at me was cross eyed or I would not be writing this today. North Vietnamese soldiers shouted in English "We're coming to get you." Kill you, kill you. We fought back, but our new M-16 rifles received earlier in the year began to break down. I was happy I had a 45 hand gun. As our fire dropped off a signal sounded on the hillside. The North Vietnamese squad leaders maneuvered their soldiers out of the bunkers to flank and over run us. They were able to isolate Marine positions. I can still remember two marines sitting back to back fighting off the fucking NVA. Their piece of shit M-16's jamming on them until the bastards got to them. It made you sick to watch. After the battle, dozens of Marines were found dead crouched over their rifles. They were killed as they tried to thread together the three separate pieces of their cleaning rods, so they could ram a jammed shell casings out of the rifles and return to the fight.

We had to pull back from the fight without our dead. A B-52 had been called in to bomb the fuck out of them. We waited as heavy artillery and massive air strikes blasted the vegetation from the hill top, then we waited while more bombs blew the splinters and soil to ugly brown goo. Then we climbed back to the top of Hill to find only silence, no NVA, no trees, nothing but dead Marines. By the time the hill was captured there were 120 Marines dead and more than 80 evacuated with wounds. Most of the dead Marines were found with their rifles torn down next to them because they didn't work. The fight for the Hill was declared a victory, ya right. However, it was a successful fight in that it prevented the small outpost of Khe Sahn from being over run.

CHAPTER 17

THANKSGIVING DINNER

I found out years later that the M-16 was strongly defended as a fine assault rifle. Marine officers in both Saigon and Washington suggested that Marines carelessness in training and maintenance had been responsible for its breakdown in battle. I read later that the US government said that the new M-16 was fool proof, but not Marine proof. The fucking butt heads. It wouldn't be until late 1967 before all the M-16's in Vietnam had been recalled, refitted with chrome chambers and a new buffer system to reduce the rate of fire. Also it was provided with a different gun powder to the lessen jamming.

The Marines of India Company were starting to replace their M-16's with the old M-14's even though it was heavier. The M-14 could reach five hundred meters from ridgeline to ridgeline with power, while the M-16 was only deadly at close range, when it did work! The NVA continued to try and run us off the top of the Hill, but was un-successful in doing it. Kind of funny when I think back as a kid, playing King of the Hill as a game. We had to dig, dig and dig deep fox holes. There were rats everywhere, some eating on dead NVA. You didn't dare to take your boots off. We weren't allowed to shoot them because we were low on ammo and someone might get hit with a stray bullet. The rats were big, about the size of a rabbit. They really didn't bother me that much although I didn't want to get bitten. The shots you had to get from being bitten were much worse than the bite. Fifteen shots in the stomach. We were going to be here for a long time so I just had to make some of them my pets. I gave them all names, Blackie, George and one of them the name of Lana, because he/she/it was mean to the others. I wonder where I got that name.

The Army 1st cavalry was starting to replace the 26th on both Hill 881 North and South. This was toward the end of November. That made me happy not only to get off the Hill, but also the Army always ate well. We got to join them for their Thanksgiving dinner. I had my Thanksgiving dinner on top of Hill 881 North with my pets. We all got one Washington grown apple and one egg, the first I had in months. One beer that I traded for a can of ham and lima beans and a piece of processed turkey. It was the best meal that I had in a long time.

Benny and me had been listening to the radio allot. It was during this time that we both realized that there were moratoriums back in the USA. These were anti-war demonstrations consisting of mostly students, teachers and some politicians. This was the era of "make love not war" and there was a considerable amount of anti war propaganda being spread around. Even in 1966. Although it got allot worse in 1967 and 68. I absolutely despised the peace marchers back in the United States, here we were in a jungle war zone without the comfort and security that they had and all they ever did was take time off from their studies to disrupt what we were fighting for and then go home at night to sleep in their comfy beds. They condemned and ridiculed us, we were simply the sacrificial pawns used by our government and abused by our fellow countrymen. The asshole people back at home didn't care if we got killed or not. Why did they think we were the bad guy's? We didn't want to be here and did they think I liked the fact that I wasn't going to heaven after all I was doing over here. You would think that the people at home would be more caring about us but they didn't care at all. Benny and I heard that on the radio time after time. Hell, I even told the Father that I didn't want to think about being a Catholic. I wasn't sure that God thought what I was doing (killing people.) was right. I still believed in God but it was hard to. Benny told me that God would look out for me and him anyway. He was a strong Catholic. Twice the man I'll ever be.

CHAPTER 18

CHRISTMAS

It was in the middle of December when we left the Hill. I said goodbye to Blackie and George. I couldn't find Lana. Probably ran off with another Marine. My recon team was transferred to the 2nd Battalion 3rd Marines. The recon force in Vietnam that I was with moved around from one hell hole to another, that's probably why I got into so much shit all the time. This time we were assigned to the Southern area of the country. The USA Marine forces were mostly in the Northern provinces where most of the fighting took place. We were really there as a political force to justify the US intervention. Each province in South Vietnam had their own groups of enemy such as the Xuen Mock guerillas and the professional Local Force Regiment D445 which were usually in Phuoc Tuy Province. So even though we were now in a more secure area in the south we still would have our hands full. The Army had their hands full also. There was more security in the South only because of the constant patrolling and search and destroy operations that were carried out.

I believe the Recon Marines were much more disciplined and better thought of (by the Marine Corps) than the regular Marines. We trained together in California and Okinawa after our basic Marine Corp and ITR training. All of this training took place before going "in country" so that when we went there we would be a complete unit. Where as the US seemed to send a bunch of

Marines to Vietnam, then split them up and sent them wherever a replacement was needed. They were all individuals and strangers to each other and the bonds of brother hood, as they call it now, that we had were uncommon among most Marines. We almost always operated in small groups attached to a company or a platoon. The Marines seemed to always send out small patrols without much support. So it was a good thing that you knew each other well, but also a bad thing when one of us was killed. We had taken on six new replacements to give us a total of ten Recon Marines again. I finally understood why no one wanted to talk to me when I first made country. I didn't talk to them unless I had to. I think still today that it's hard for me to make new friends. It seems like every time you love someone or become close, they go away on you. It was during this time that I received a letter from my friend Duane's mom. He was killed by a NVA rocket. He was a gunner on a chopper. Everyone along with him was killed. At first I didn't know how to feel about the lost of my friend. I had seen so many young Marines die by then that I was becoming hard. It wasn't until two nights later when I was on watch all alone that I broke down and cried like a baby.

We started to run recon patrols every other day and would set up ambushes at night along a rice paddy or on a small hill over looking villages. I can still remember something that happened during this time at Christmas. It was on Christmas Eve when Cpl. Cain, Reed, Benny and me and three other Marines were ordered to go on a recon mission near an ARVN (Army of the Republic of Vietnam) outpost. We were to start out in the afternoon, patrol for five miles and then hold up at a village until night fall to set up an ambush till morning, (Christmas morning.) I remember while at the village everyone talking about Christmas back home and what their families did on Christmas Eve. I started thinking about popcorn balls and how my brother and I used to hang popcorn strings on the tree. Poor people understand popcorn strings. I thought to myself what a bunch of crap having to sit in an ambush all night. I asked one of the new guys what he thought about it and his reply was, well you know what they say U.S.M.C. (You Suckers Miss Christmas.) I looked at him strangely, but when he smiled at me I couldn't help but smile back. The night was long and I did allot of thinking about Christmas. I even wondered what Santa might bring me. Maybe some new bullets for my 45, mine were turning green. Maybe even that popcorn ball I couldn't get out of my mind.

In the morning just at dawn we all got ready to move out back to camp, but before we left we ate some of our rations. The thing I will always remember is that one of the other new guys got up from where he was sitting, walked over to a bush and stuck a can on top of it. Then he took out a pack of cigarettes, tore off some of the foil and put it on the bush. It wasn't long before all of us started putting things on the bush. The bush looked like hell. Then this same guy who was about six foot three and about 220 pounds started singing silent night. At first I thought how goofy, but then I started singing it too. We all sang the song twice and then we stopped just as suddenly as we had all started. We picked up our gear and moved out.

While leaving I looked back at that bush and thought that's one of the most beautiful Christmas trees I had ever seen. I guess it doesn't matter what worldly possessions you have in life, it's the family and friends you have or have had, now gone to another place. It's a sad thing that men had to die on Christmas Eve. It makes me think of the one who died for all of us so that we might live. Our Lord, "Jesus Christ."

Well Christmas morning came and went almost unnoticed. I didn't get the popcorn ball, hell I didn't even get the bullets. I did get the next two days to rest though. After a couple of days rest my recon team received orders to board choppers and land at a place called An Dinh.We were to reinforce with a platoon from Delta Company 3/26 to attack the village of An Dinh, which was connected to a village south of Gia Binh. The village of An Dinh is located east of Con Thien. We were to advance on the village due to reports that the village was full of NVA. When we were sent in for a reconnaissance we became heavily engaged by the NVA. I called for supporting arms (105 mm artillery rounds) to saturate the area. Delta Company followed up with an attack but again ran into heavy fire. Air strikes were called in and produced secondary explosions. At around midday Delta Company again entered the village and found trenches and tunnels. About two hours later the Company became under fire with heavy automatic weapons, so air strikes had to be called in again. The company pulled back and waited for the air strikes. After the air strikes Delta Company advanced again and we conduct a reconnaissance. It was getting late in the afternoon and the area looked to be secure, so Delta Company entered the village once again. We came under heavy automatic weapons fire from both of our flanks and we were pinned down. I called for artillery once again and finally contact with the NVA was broken. The village was taken and made secure. We would remain in the village until December 31st removing weapons and food left by the NVA. We started moving the villagers and animals out of the village as fast I we could. At around 23 hundred hours on the 31st of December the village was burnt to the ground. I spent New Years Eve on a chopper.

CHAPTER 19

HILL 861

I had hoped that the New Year would bring better times, at least start out without any NVA or VC trying to kill us. It wasn't to be. It was around 0130 (1:30 AM) Jan 1st 1967 as we reached our new base camp at Camp Carol. All of a sudden a couple of rounds hit our chopper but no one was hit. One of the other choppers wasn't so lucky. Two Marines were hit. The wounds didn't kill them, but they were fucked up. When we landed Cpl.Cain told Benny, Reed and me to grab the other guys on the recon team and stay together while he reported into the CP. We were now with the 9th Marines. We were transferred there because a force recon team from the 9th needed recon support. The contact with the NVA was becoming more and more frequent again around hill 861, hill 881 North and South. Hell, we were just there a couple of months ago. Four Marine gun ships (helicopters) were lost to small arms fire a couple of weeks earlier and eleven Marines lost their lives. With the recon team from 1/9 reporting a big build up of fortifications and NVA activity around the bottom of Hill 861. The 9th Marines were going to have to secure the bottom of the hill once again. While the 2nd Bn 26th Marines ran patrols down from the top of the hill. Hill 861 was about 1500 meters west of the airstrip being built at Khe Sanh. The NVA needed the hills because they over looked the Khe Sanh base.

Cpl. Cain returned with good old SSgt. Henry. I didn't like him very much because he was always shooting his mouth off. When we were on patrol he would say things like spread it out! Spread it out! If one round comes in it will kill all of you. Then he would say I don't care if you get killed, I just don't want to write that many letters home to your mommies. Of course he was right we were trained to make sure that there was a least five meters between each Marine just for that purpose, however he could have left off the mommy's part. Cpl. Cain and SSgt. Henry had talked to the base commander who was convinced there was little or no NVA presence or activity even though the recon teams were reporting there was around Khe Sanh, including Hills 881-North and South and 861. What the hell was he thinking! During the brief with the Khe Sanh commander (who was a Captain,) the LT in charge of the recon teams reported numerous bunkers, lots of enemy and recommended the hills be subject to many, many hours of prepping with air strikes. Then with artillery firing a barrage of 105mm rounds the 9th Marines could advance some 1000 meters behind. Cpl. Cain told us that the Captain looked around and said, 'Bullshit!' he wasn't going to waste the fire power. The LT. looked at SSgt. Henry and said, 'Well, Staff Sergeant Henry, our briefing is completed.' They turned around and walked out of there. What a dumb ass Captain. He would cost the Marines a lot of lives in the next couple of weeks when the 9th Marines, Golf Company was sent up Hill 861.

This would be the second time I was wounded. Cpl. Cain led us over to where the bunkers were, it would be where we would run our Recon patrols from. Two days later at 0300 (3:00 am) Golf Company along with my Recon team was ordered to advance up Hill 861. I couldn't believe there wasn't one sign of the enemy. The night before there were allot of guy's writing letters home and talking about getting killed. I even thought to myself that maybe this was it for me also. Just as we reached the top of the hill I stated thinking about what a goof I was to be so worried the night before. Well, just as the point man reached the crest of the hill he was hit in the neck with what looked like a 50 caliber round because his head almost came completely off. I hit the ground fast just as AK47 rounds started flying through the air.

Damn! We'd walked into a company size ambush. The NVA were hiding in spider traps that you couldn't see. Up and out they came screaming in English "kill you! kill you!"

I took off my radio because it had the twenty foot whip antenna on it instead of the normal five foot tape antenna. The twenty foot was for longer distance. It made me an easy target for snipers. There was a Sgt standing next to me; I never did know his name, a couple of hand grenades landed next to him and me. I was already down so I only took a hit in the arm, in the neck and in the side with a couple of small pieces of shrapnel. The Sgt wasn't so lucky. His left leg was blown off from above his knee. Even though he must have been in sever pain and in shock he still directed fire and gave orders. He stuck the bloody stub of his leg into the ground to help stop the bleeding. I was going to help him, but he told me to give him the receiver of my radio so that he could talk to one of the other platoons. We were with the second platoon. First and Third Platoons were operating just west of Hill 861 about 1000 meters from us. We were supposed to provide a defensive position incase 1st and 3rd platoon run into trouble.Well they did run into trouble and so did we.

CHAPTER 20

IN HIS EYES

It was at this time that I would kill a man while looking him in the eyes. It was a lot different than just shooting in the dark or at a group of NVA and killing them. He was yelling and shooting at me and I could see by the look on his face he was as scared as I was. I fired my 45 what seemed to be five times before I hit him. The round blew a hole in his chest and he flew backwards about four feet. I had a load of adrenalin pumping through my veins and ran screaming at him. I got there just as the blood started pouring out of his mouth and he looked up at me. He knew he was dead and he knew who had killed him. He was just a kid about eighteen, so was I but looking back at it now he hasn't changed, he's still that eighteen year old that I killed. Even though I would go on to kill again and again I'll always remember the feeling I had on that day when I killed someone's son. I still see him in my nightmares.

By this time a corpsman was putting bandages on the Sgt's leg or at least what was left of it and he had passed out from the pain. Cpl Cain took over the radio. There were so many Marines and NVA running around shooting and yelling at each other it seemed like a circus. For just a moment everything was moving in slow motion. The Sgt had called in artillery support and the 26th Marines had come to the rescue from the Northwest part of the hill. 1st and 3rd platoon was taking a beating from rockets. Just about then I heard Benny yelling at me to come on let's go. Cpl Cain through his M16 to me and said you two lay down some fire on the right flank. I ran over to Benny and hit the ground. On the way over to him I could feel the bullets passing close by my face. What a strange feeling, too hard to describe. It was just a moment later when Reed hit the ground next to us. For some strange reason I felt happy that both of them were there with me. If I was going to die let it be with them by my side. We opened up on the right flank just like Cpl Cain had ordered us to and it wasn't long before the first artillery support that the Sgt had called for, started coming in. The ground shook and dirt flew through the air along with big rocks and pieces of shrapnel. Benny yelled let's get the hell out of here and we dropped back down the hill about twenty meters. There was a big hole, probably a bomb crater so we all jumped into it. There was a bloody leg lying in the hole. It belonged to a NVA soldier because his boot that looked like a tennis shoe was still on his foot. He either got completely blown away or hobbled away on one leg because he was no where to be found. Normally if someone is able to get up or crawl away they take their body parts with them, for all the good it does. I saw that more than once. I guess when your in shock you do thing's that only one can imagine.

Four gunship's (choppers) from the Army 1st Calvary showed up. The artillery support had done the job, the NVA were falling back to the east side of the hill. The gunship's had a field day. They had them in the open and were ripping them a new asshole. I couldn't see much of it but found out later that they had many kills. Most of the fighting was over so I told Benny I was going back over to Cpl Cain so that I could start calling in medi-vacs. The hill had been taken back again, but not without heavy casualties.

CHAPTER 21

THE MUSIC

There would be more fighting for the next twelve days before Gulf Company and my recon team could return to base camp. I was fine so I told Cpl. Cain I didn't need to get medical help for myself until we got back to base camp. Actually I should have gone with the others because a small piece of shrapnel went all the way through my arm and the wound was infected by the time we got back. Hurt like hell when they cleaned out the wound. The Doc had to dig deep into my arm to clean it. I deserved it for trying to be the tough Marine. I must have thought I was John Wayne or Sgt York. Later that night and for the next couple of days I couldn't sleep very well, not just because my arm and neck hurt, but thing's kept running through my head about the thing's that had happened. I wrote in my diary about the dumb ass Captain and how he needlessly caused so many Marines to die, because of his arrogance. I wrote that someone should have fragged him. To bad he wasn't in the battle, must be nice just to sit back at base camp and give the orders. I also wrote about the man I killed. I thought about his Mother and what went through her head when she found out about his death. It was easy to think that Viet nesses don't have feelings because that's how I was trained, but all people everywhere have feelings and all soldiers must be bothered sometime in their life about the thing's they have done. Maybe it's when you get to be an old man like I am now, when you start to reflect on it.

Benny and Reed wanted me to go to one of the other bunkers with them. There was a party going on for a couple of Marines that were going home. Their tour of duty in this God forgotten country was over. I was a little jealous of them, but not for long. There was a few of Navy Seabees at the party and they brought beer. The Seabees always had beer. I drank one and started feeling better, besides Benny and a couple of the other guy's were singing to a 45 rpm record that was playing on the record player. The song was the 1964 hit by The Temptations, My Girl. The two other guys singing with Benny were Black or is it (African American now,) anyway they sounded great. It wasn't long before more guys joined in singing. That one song has been played in more Vietnam War movies than any other song that I can remember. They also played a new song just released in 1966 called the Ballad of the Green Berets by SSgt Barry Sadler, you know, fighting soldiers from the sky, fearless men who jump and die, men who mean just what they say, the brave men of the Green Berets...etc etc. Being a grunt Marine you learn to live with what you got and it's the little things like being together singing to some records that meant more to me than having a Million dollars at the time. It's like they say..." it's 1, 2, 3, 4, what are we fighting for. Don't ask me, I don't give a damn! Next stop is Vietnam.

I was really into Soul music at the time, maybe because the songs were about love and tenderness, like another song by the Temptations "It's Growing". The music gave me peace of mind, even if it was for a short time. Even today I can see the smile on Benny's face, singing to My Girl. I sure miss him. After a couple of more beers and a little singing myself I was really tired. I was glad I didn't have watch that night, I never would have made it. I went back to our hole and fell asleep; finally I was at peace with myself.

Chapter 22

Easter

When Easter 1967 came Benny and me hid hand grenades, after all we didn't have any eggs. We put packs of cigarettes on them out of our C-rations. One of the grenades had a whole pack of Winston's on it that was sort of the golden egg. It was a lot of fun doing it and watching some of the guys looking for them. I hadn't started smoking yet so I always traded my cigarettes for food or would give them away. Benny and I gave thanks to Lord and prayed that He would watch over our fellow Marines and our families back at home.

Throughout the remaining months of January through part of May of 1967, my recon team and the 9th Marines conducted numerous search and destroy operations to search out the NVA while trying to strengthen our civic action programs. We tried to secure relations with the Vietnamese people and free the people from the constant threat of the VC (Viet Cong) as well as the NVA. Some of the major operations during this time were called, Root Beer, Mississippi Mud, Cleveland, and Independence. One of the biggest and most significant was Operation Mississippi Mud in the Antenna Valley, where the 9th Marine units captured sixty tons of rice and relocated around 2,500 Vietnamese refugees.

In May, the regiment moved to Dong Ha. I was happy about that because the 26th Marines 3/26 of the 5th division had just got there a few days before us and

Benny and I could go find Chino. We hadn't seen him for a long. Well we found him when we landed at Dong Ha and unloaded our gear, but we wouldn't have long to visit him. He was being transferred down South to the 3rd Marines because of his expertise in explosives. We got to talk to him for about thirty minutes and then he was gone. I would never see him again, but I'm sure he made it home. I never did know his last name. I still regret that today. I was starting to get to know some of the other guys on the recon team. Still there was only Cpl. Cain, Benny, Reed and me that hung around each other, but it was hard not to get close to a couple of the other guys. One of the guys I started to talk to more and more was a Catholic just like me. His name was Berry Stevens. He was just a little guy around five foot five inches and one hundred and twenty pounds, if that. Not that being small mattered, because that's about how big Audie Murphy was. Audie Murphy had gone on to win among his **33 awards** and decorations, the coveted **Congressional Medal of Honor**, the highest military award for bravery that can be given to any individual in the United States of America, for "conspicuous gallantry and intrepidity at the risk of his life above and beyond the call of duty." He also received every decoration for valor that his country had to offer, some of them more than once, including 5 decorations by France and Belgium. He was the most decorated soldier of World War II, and he wasn't even a Marine. Born June 20th 1924, I was born June 20th 1948. He died in a plane crash on May 28th 1971 at age 46. He is still my hero.

CHAPTER 23

DONG HA

Berry would be my backup Recon Radioman even though he wasn't Recon. There were so many radiomen being blown apart or killed that sometimes you had to use squad or platoon radiomen as backups. That's how we got him on our team. We started sharing the radio responsibly as soon as I knew I could depend on him, which wasn't long. By now I had been in Vietnam for Eleven months and he was a boot to country. I was an old veteran to him even though I was only eighteen. Marines usually have two tours of duty, thirteen months each. I was getting close to the end of my first duty. Then it would be back to the real world for six months and then back to this hell hole for another thirteen months. I wasn't sure what I was going to do. Go home and back again or just re-up since I was already here.

It was about this time that the R&R's (rest and relaxation) started coming in but I didn't take any. I guess I just wasn't sure what I wanted to do. Sex, since I had never had any before didn't seem to be a big deal to me. I was more interested in eating so I would trade my R&R's to guy's for part of their C-rations. I knew what it was like not to have something to eat! I'm glad I didn't die a virgin over there, never knowing what it felt like to have a women making love to me. I would find that out within the next few weeks and wish I had my R&R's back.

During late May and through the last week of July we ran six man recon patrols out of Dong Ha. In June I turned nineteen and Benny gave me a candy bar he got from home. It was a chocolate Hershey bar and I shared it with him and Berry. On July 4th we listened to Hanoi Hannah on the radio asking why we were celebrating the United States Birthday when our country didn't care about us and why were the black soldiers fighting when they didn't have the same rights the white people had. I have to admit in a way that made sense to me. There were a few fire fights but nothing big or anything that I witnessed to write about in my diary, until July 27th. We ran a recon patrol out of a CAP unit, sometimes called CAC unit (Combined Action Platoon.) CAP units consisted of about twenty to twenty-five Marines and Corpsman at a time. The Marines and Corpsmen of the CAP/CAC units attempted to isolate the people of select villages from the NVA, VC and the ravages of the war. CAP villages were no longer targets of the indiscriminate Marine search and destroy missions so prevalent during the Vietnam War.

The Marines shared the risk of living in the villages twenty-four hours a day trying to earn the love and respect of thousands of villagers who simply wanted to survive a war they didn't want. They communicated with the villagers about farming and helped with any of the medical concerns the villagers had. The CAP/CAC unit was a compound on one end of the village with the perimeter surrounded by concertina barbed wire. The CAP Marines would run day and night patrols from there. On the 27th we went with one of their day patrols leaving around fifteen Marines in the compound. We had traveled about 1000 meters from the CAP unit when we heard an explosion which sounded like it came from the CAP unit. We started back in a force march and sent out a couple of point men just to make sure we didn't walk into an ambush. It took around forty minutes to get back to the village. What we found was a nightmare. All the CAP Marines were dead along with some of the villagers. Some of the Marines were thrown up on the barb wire with their throats cut and their eyes gouged out. Some of them were burned so badly that their own Mothers wouldn't have been able to identify them. It was sickening to see it. I hated being in this God forgotten country and I wondered if I would ever get over what I had seen during my time in country.

My recon team was flying out of Dong Ha on H-46 helicopters. Dong Ha was the Marine staging area for ongoing battles in the mountains, hills and the jungles to the west. Most of the trips were day trips. We would leave at 0500 hrs (5am) and return again by H-46's around 1900 hrs (7pm). We would be dropped in an open field or elephant grass and force march to a location that only Cpl Cain knew, to setup an OP (outpost) for reconnaissance. I hated the elephant grass. It was about eight feet tall and very thick. Once you got dropped off in it you had to stay together or you could get lost in it. That happened more than once. You had to start yelling to fine someone, oh great, just what you needed when your trying to stay concealed from the NVA. The grass also had slimy black stuff on it that got all over your hands and face as well as your uniform. I found out years later that it was a chemical call agent-orange used to kill the vegetation on the ground, like elephant grass.

On one of our recon OP's we held up on top of a hill over looking a valley. There was a lot of vegetation so we were hidden from view. Early that morning there wasn't any activity to report but by 1300 hrs the area came to life. There were a couple of squads of Marines from 3/26 on patrol in the valley below us. We didn't see them because they were just out of view from where we were. They had stopped at a bomb crater to take baths and had some chow. The bomb craters always had water in them due to the rain. The water was always dirty but what the hell. Anyway, the NVA had one of their recon teams hidden in the jungle on the side of the other hill across from us. They opened up on the Marines with 82mm mortar rounds that hit the target. We could see the smoke from the mortar tube so it made it easier to call in artillery support. In the mean time there were some of the Marines running down the road in the valley naked holding their gear and uniforms in their arms. It would have been funny to watch except for the fact that some of them were bleeding from the shrapnel wounds they received.

We had a sniper with us, his name was James Dewitt. We all called him Dutch. He was so good with his M14 rifle. It had a sniper scope on it and he could hit anything big or small from well over 500 meters away. He told me to watch this and he shot a round in the direction of the white smoke coming from the mortar tube. The mortar rounds stopped for a few seconds and Dutch told me that he knew just where to shoot to kill the loader of the tube. Another mortar round came out and Dutch shot again. The rounds stopped for about thirty seconds and then all of a sudden the rounds were coming at us. We had been spotted. Two or three rounds came in before our support artillery started to hit around the area of the NVA. A couple of rounds hit the target and it was over. The Marines suffered some wounds but I found out later that no one died or was seriously hurt.

Chapter 24

R & R

It was getting close to the end of my first tour of duty. I only had a couple of weeks to go and I had to decide what I was going to do. Go home or re-up for another thirteen months. Benny helped me make the decision. I had forgotten that he had been in country one month longer than me and he had already decided to stay. He was already on his second tour and had said nothing about it. Besides there was so much protesting going on back home and I just didn't want to deal with it. Also to be honest about it I wasn't sure how I would feel about coming back after six months. It wouldn't be the first time that someone decided to take off to another country rather than have to face going again. I don't think I would have done that, but who really knows. If you re-up to stay you can pick the unit you want to serve with. He stayed with us and he told me that he hoped that I would stay also. Benny took an R&R a while back, but I just thought it was his normal R&R. When you re-up you get an R&R almost right away, so I decided to stay and asked if there were any R&R's available. There were two, one to Bancock Thailand and the other to Kuala Lumpur the capital of Malaysia. I took Malaysia. I also picked up another rank. I was now an E4 Cpl (corporal.) You make fast rank in a combat zone, if you stay alive long enough.

I flew into Da Nang two days later, found my sea bag and pulled out my uniform. I looked like hell, but so did

all the other guys who were going on R&R. It didn't matter how you looked, only that you were in uniform. When
I got to Malaysia I had to board a bus from the airport
along with everyone else who was staying at the same hotel I was. The military makes you stay at certain hotels
that they have checked out as ok and they make sure that
the girls (prostitutes) at the hotels are clean from any VD
(venereal disease).You couldn't have guys coming back
to combat sick or with VD. I think that was a good thing.
As soon as I arrived at the hotel I gave the money I drew
from my combat savings to the manager who put in the
safe after I checked in. I kept some of the money even
though I really didn't know how much I had. When the
military gives you your money for your R&R they give
you the money from the country you're going to. I had
Malaysian money. At that time the American dollar was
worth four times theirs. I took four hundred American
dollars, so that was sixteen hundred dollars. That was a
lot of money.

I had just got to my room and was looking around
when there was a knock on the door. When I opened it
there was a Malaysian man standing there with a rack of
clothes. I let him in and bought a couple pairs of slacks
and a couple of shirts. He even had shoes, socks, and
underwear. There were a couple of them going room
to room selling clothes. I thought that's kind of cool,
I didn't even have to go out to find a shop. As soon as he
left there was another knock on the door. Standing there
was another Malaysian man. He introduced himself as a
cab driver who could speak English, Japanese and Malaysian. He wanted to know if I wanted to hire him for the
five days, four nights that I would be in Kuala Lumpur.

I asked him to wait right there and I went to the room next to mine. There was an Army guy there and I asked him what all this was about. He said, I can see you have never been on R&R before have you. After I told him no, he said hire him and he will take care of you. Then he told me how much to pay the guy and if there was a problem to come back over and he would talk to him. I went back to my room and we agreed on a price. Now I had a room, clothes, and a cab driver to drive me around. He told me that he would wait down in the lobby for me until after I got dressed and that his name was Kamal. As he was leaving there was still another knock on the door. I thought to myself, what now. There stood another Malaysian man but not by himself. He had five young ladies with him that looked Malaysian and Japanese. He wanted to know if I wanted buy any of them for the week. Kamal told him no, no, no as he was pushing them out the door. Actually I wanted them all. I wasn't sure what I would do with them, but they were beautiful. Wow, my world was moving fast and I was starting to feel like a big shot. Kamal went down to the lobby and waited while I got dressed.

When I came down I asked him if he could take me somewhere to eat. He did and waited outside in the cab for me even though I asked him if he wanted to eat with me. After I had my meal he took me around to different areas to look at women. I guess I was acting kind of funny because he asked me if I ever made love to a girl. I told him no and that I was a little scared. He smiled and said no problem I know where to take you. He took me to a place that looked like a nightclub. We went into the back room and there were girls standing with other soldiers. He said you pick and I talk to the owner. I looked around at some of the women, but I could see that most of them looked like they were already taken. Then I saw one that I really liked and told my driver that I would like to have her. I didn't know how old she was because all of them looked young. When he said something to the owner the owner looked as though he got mad. Kamal came over to me and said she not for sell, she daughter, she sixteen, she not one of these girls. I told him to please tell the owner that I was sorry and that I didn't mean any disrespect. The owner must have forgiven me because he said you pick girl now and only pay this much as he was counting his fingers. I had no idea how much he wanted. I picked another girl but she was just finishing up with another guy and I would have to wait two days. Kamal said no, no, no I take you someplace and I think you like girl I show you. She much money but not like these girls, only have soldiers sometimes. I guess he meant that she didn't have a solder every week. Then I wondered how much she was going to cost me. Then I figured who cares this might be the only chance I had to find out what sex was all about. Then I thought to myself, she may not want me. I tried not to think anymore, my brain was starting to hurt.

Kamal took me down town to a building that looked like it had four or five stories to it. We went up to the top floor and he knocked on the door. I heard a voice call to come in. Kamal told me to wait right here. I waited by a sliding door that opened up to a baloney. There were flowers everywhere and a nice view. Then I heard Kamal say turn this way. When I did I couldn't believe my eyes. There stood a beautiful Japanese girl dressed in a long white dress that went to the floor. She had one strap over her shoulder and her other shoulder was bare. The top of her dress came down to her breast. She was holding a martini glass with one hand and her other arm was raised above her head against the door to her bedroom. I could feel the blood rushing through my body and I felt like I was going to pass out. Kamal said this is Suki Kim Niou. I didn't know what to do, so like an idiot I just stood there and started moving my head up and down. Finally Kamal introduced me and I shook her hand. I thought the other girls I had seen were beautiful, but she looked like an actress. She was about five foot and looked like she was 105 pounds. She had long black hair down to the middle of her back and deep dark brown eyes. Her face was so great looking that it took my breath away. They both started speaking in Japanese so I had no idea what they were talking about. It looked and sounded to me like she wasn't too trilled about the idea of her and me. Finally Kamal said to me ok we go now. When we got back in the cab I said where do we go now? He said we go to hotel, she come. I said oh, I thought she didn't like me. He said no, no, no, she like you very much, she like your face, but she asks what soldier you are. I tell her a Marine. When I tell her that she not like it. She think all Marines crazy in head because of war. They always mean to her, not like Airman or Navy. They! always nice to her. I asked him, then why did she pick me? He said I tell her that you baby, never have girl before. She like that and you have nice face.

He dropped me off at the hotel and I went up to my room after I had a couple of drinks. It was so weird being able to order a drink. I was only nineteen and back in the real world (USA) you had to be twenty-one. Its still twenty-one today but the voting age has changed from twenty-one to eighteen. I think that's a good thing because how could you fight and die for your country and yet not even vote for the people sending you off to war. I laid down on the bed with my head spinning. I was thinking about her and wondering if I was going to make a fool out of myself. I didn't even know how much I was supposed to pay her although it didn't matter to me. I would have given her all the money I had, just to be with her for one night. I got up and walked over to the door to go out into the hallway when there was a knock on the door. I open the door and there she was. She had on a different dress that went to just above her knees and she was holding a large bag. I asked her in and shut the door. I asked her if she spoke English and she said yes, "I speak English and understand". She put her bag down and asked me how old I was. I said nineteen. Like the idiot I was, I asked her how old she was. After I did I felt like a real dumb ass. She said twenty-five. Wow! I thought to myself, twenty-five. My first time was going to be with a older women. My heart started pounding again. She then walked over to the door and locked it, turned around and walked back over to me. She put her hands on my shoulders, reached up and kissed me on the lips. She unbuttoned my shirt and pulled it off. She kissed my chest and pulled her hands from my shoulders down across my chest. Then she un-did my pants and pulled them down and I stepped out of them. She stepped back and took all of her clothes off while I stood there watching her. She was so beautiful I couldn't believe it. She took my hand and led me to the bathroom where she started to fill the tub with warm water. I was getting so embarrassed my face was turning red. She turned around and went out of the bathroom to get something from her bag. I watched her as she left. Man she had a nice butt. She looked good all over, front and back.

When she returned the tub was just about full. She pulled my shorts off and told me to get into the tub and stand there. Then she got in and turned off the water. She faced me, took a bar of soap and started to wash me down from my neck to my thighs. I was supposed to be a fighting Marine, but in her hands I was a bowl of Jell-O. She rinsed me off and told me to sit down. I did and she got on her knees and started kissing me again. All of a sudden she was sitting on top me. This is what I had been waiting nineteen years for. I couldn't believe I had wasted my R&R's for food. She worked me over until I thought my head was going to explode. I think I lasted thirty seconds. I laid my head on her breast with my arms around her. She took my head in her hands and looked me in the eyes. She said something that I will never forget. She said you just baby and no have girl before. So you no make love good. That OK, because I teach you make good love to girl. I guess I should have been angry but I had no idea what the hell she was talking about. I felt great!

We spent the next four days going to lunch and dinner and nightclubs. Kamal drove us around so that she could show me the city. I loved sight seeing with her, but I wanted the nights to never end. Just as she had promised, she taught me things that I have never forgotten. She taught me how to make love to a women in the way she wanted, not the way I wanted. She would tell me things like you make love to girl before and after. You hold her and talk to her. I didn't know that women were supposed to enjoy it just like men and that they needed to be satisfied. I was glad I waited. The last night I was with her I wanted it to last forever. We got very little sleep. The next morning I had to start getting ready to go back to that hell hole. We talked over breakfast about how I was going to miss her. She told me that she was afraid for me. At the hotel while I was waiting with the other guy's for the bus to take us to the airport, I sat on a bench close to the front of the doors. She sat there with me and laid her head on my shoulder. We talked about how she got started in this kind of business. She told me it was the money. She said she used to work in a store. I thought about what she meant when she said the money and then I realized that she was right. The money was good! I paid her one thousand dollars for five days. That was a lot of money but what the hell. I wasn't sure I was going to make it home anyway and it was worth it to me. I told her that I thought I was in love with her. She said you not in love with me. All boy's think they in love their first time. You go back to war and then go home. You marry American girl and then you forget about Suki. She took out a pair of red laced panties and a picture of her. She handed them to me and said this make you remember Suki long time. The bus pulled up and my heart started pounding again. She kissed me on the neck and then on the lips. I turned around and got on the bus. When I sat down I waved at her and she waved back. After the bus pulled away from the hotel I looked back out through the back window and I saw Suki put her face in her hands. I think she was sobbing. I really couldn't figure out way, was it because I was headed back to a war and that I might be killed? Maybe she liked me more than I thought. I wished that I had more time to talk to her and ask her how she really felt. Was I just another soldier with money in his pocket or was there really something between us. I'll never know, because that was the last time I would ever see again. She was right; I went back to Nam and finally made it home. I married an American girl just as she said I would. I still think about her from time to time even after all these years. I sometimes wonder if she ever married or has ever thought about me over the last forty-one years. I wonder if she is still alive. I hope she is happy where ever she is. I will never forget her for as long as I live.

Chapter 25

Shake & Bake

When I got back to Da-Nang I reported in and then went to the storage building to pack away my uniform and the clothes I had bought. The last thing I put in my sea bag was her picture. I held it in my hand and looked at it for a long time before putting it away. After I stored my gear I went to find out when I was to report back to my unit. Six hours later I was on my way back to Dong Ha. I was happy to see Benny and Reed. Cpl.Cain was out on patrol so I didn't see him until the next day. When I did he asked me, well how was it. I said I had a good time. He said you know what I mean! I looked at Benny and he smiled at me. I smiled back and said to all of them it was the greatest; I hope it won't be my last. They all teased me for two days. We also picked up a new LT (2nd lieutenant) he was a real shake and bake "Shake & Bake" was slang for quickly trained commissioned officers during the Vietnam War. They were officers straight out of OCS (officer candidate school) with no combat training. "Well" we didn't hit it off very well right from the start. It wasn't because he was a boot to country. It was because he acted like I was. He was there one day before I got back from my R&R. He asked me question after question about my radio skills and map reading, and how often I changed the batteries in my radio. All of this would have been ok with me if he hadn't acted like a big shot. He should have just shut up and let the Sgt and Cpl's handle thing's until he learned a few thing's, hell I was a Cpl myself, but I guess he wanted everyone to know who was in charge.

The next morning we had a five mile patrol. We hadn't gone more than three miles when this dumb ass started running through the jungle like a mad man looking for water. He was popping salt tables like crazy and I told him not to. I offered him my water because he already drank his. He wouldn't take any, which really pissed me off. Finally he became weak and Cpl Cain told me to call in a medivac for him. We got him to a clearing and poured water all over him. He had heat stroke. I called for the medivac, but before it came I took out my 45 cal put it against his forehead and I told him that I should blow your fucking head off for not taking my water. What the fuck is your problem, my water isn't good enough for you. Cpl Cain told me to knock it off. He can't hear you anyway. He was lucky that day and I guess I was too. The LT was medivaced out and we finished the patrol. I never did hear what happened to him. Most LT's didn't last to long for one reason or another.

CHAPTER 26

HILL 875

We were still flying out of Dong Ha for outpost duty and recon patrols, however; we were now staying out in the field for a couple of days at a time to setup ambushes at night. This continued through Sept until the third week of October. That was when the 9th Marines along with my recon team were transferred south to support the 173rd Army Airborne 2nd battalion which had been fighting for months for control over Vietnam's Central highlands. One of the hills that they were fighting for was Hill 875. Hill 875 was a strategic hilltop that over looked one of the main routes from the Ho Chi Mihn Trail into South Vietnam. Intelligence had spotted large numbers of NVA troops on Hill 875. Hill 875 ran along a small ridgeline near the Cambodian border. The 173rd Airborne was ordered in to slow or stop the flow of enemy troops in the area. The 173rd 2nd BN was ordered to advance up the north slope of Hill 875. Air strikes were called in on the hill top in an effort to dislodge the NVA. Unfortunately the NVA was always well entrenched, NVA troops in the highlands knew how to hide.

My recon team was dropped about one mile from hill 875 for a reconnaissance mission to gather any information on NVA troop movement. We came upon what looked like a NVA base camp. It looked large. There were no NVA in sight, but there was still smoke coming out of the fire pits and they looked fresh. There were communication wires everywhere. All the supply's were gone except for some bandages and what looked like an aid station. I didn't like being there, but Cpl Cain said this is important, so we stayed long enough to gather as much information as possible without being discovered. The 9th had landed about five miles to the west of us and were going to meet us at a check point half way between our location and theirs. Due to what we had found it was decided that they would meet us at the deserted camp site. Cpl Cain called into the CP and gave them the information that we gathered and the information was forwarded to everyone concerned, I believe the 173rd army 2nd and 4th Bn was also notified.

After the 9th Marines caught up with us we set out toward hill 875. The 173rd was going to attack the hill early the next morning. It was late November 1967. I remember hearing although I didn't witness it, the 173rd had a Catholic mass service before the assault and that even non Catholics attended it. They must have been very apprehensive about it and for good reason. We could hear the fighting going on in the early hours of the morning. There was artillery and air strikes smashing down the top of the hill. By this time we were about one half mile from the hill. The 173rd fought a big battle that lasted from the 19th through the 22nd. On the 23rd helicopters flew in hot turkey dinners for the survivors of the battle. They had taken the hill. It was one of the bloodiest battles that the Army had fought in Vietnam. I wrote about it later in my diary along with what happened to us.

CHAPTER 27

THE 968TH NVA

During that same time the 19th through the 22nd the 9th Marines had fought its own battles. At the time of the 173rd assault up the hill, we ran into our own shit. We had two companies and we ran into a battalion of NVA from the 968th Infantry Division. They were one of North Vietnams best units. They always were blowing bugles every time they went into battle. You could never tell where the sound was coming from, in front of you or behind you. It was un-nerving as hell. I would face this unit again at Khe Sanh. This was something that our Captain or other officers hadn't planned for. The 968th was very well trained and were blood thirsty fighters. That was probably who the 173rd was facing on the hill. All we could do was setup a long defensive perimeter line and hope for the best. We were out numbered probably eight men to one.

All of a sudden we were being hit with NVA mortar rounds, B40 rockets and RPG's (rocket propelled gre-nade) an un-guided rocket equipped with an explosive warhead, made in Russia, go figure. They had us pinned down. When the first rockets hit they were on target. They landed right on top of one of our M60 machine gun placements. After the smoke cleared from the explo-sion I heard screaming. I looked up and saw a marine staggering out of the smoke. His arm was gone leaving only sinews of tissue, muscle and bone hanging down.

Two others were dead and three others had bad shrapnel wounds. Doc Billy hurried over with a couple other Marines and started working on them. I was talking on the radio to firebase 16 and asked for support. Cpl Cain gave me the drop point for the F4 phantom jet pilots. More rockets and RPG's came in and blew the hell out of us. We were in heavy brush and grass. There were trees to the side and a couple over some of the Marines. When I looked up I saw body parts hanging down. There were so many thing's running through my head at the time I had to wipe my hand across my face. I started getting mad as hell and screamed you mother fuckers. A few yards away there were nine or ten Marines who had sustained shrapnel wounds on their legs and arms.

We couldn't fall back because there was no place to go and besides there were too many wounded to move. Benny showed up just then, looked at me and said, man were fucked. I heard the bugles and I knew the NVA were coming. One of the platoon Staff Sergeants showed up with about fifteen other Marines with an M60 machine gun. His name was SSgt Steer and I was happy to see the M60. It had the fire power of 3000 rounds per minute. One hundred meters away I could see the little bastards coming. I had been in a lot of fire fights, but I had never seen anything like this before. "Well" we opened up on them and they opened up on us. There were some many rounds flying in the air I was surprised I didn't get hit. We were screaming at each other and shooting these little assholes, but they just kept coming. All of a sudden they stopped advancing about seventy meters from us. Then we heard the F4 coming in. I was happy to see it coming but I was afraid, because the NVA were dam close to us.

I wasn't sure what the hell he was going to drop. I had seen what a five hundred pound bomb could do and even worst than that, what napalm could do. I had seen the after effects of napalm and it was sickening.

Cpl Cain fired off an illumination flare in the direction of the NVA. That was so that the F4 pilot would know where to drop its load. The NVA tried to over run us but we were able to stop their advance with the help of the M60. I saw the F4 and it was coming in low, the sound filled the air. Then I saw the bomb drop from the jet, it looked like a five hundred pound bomb. We all dug our heads in and as much of our bodies as we could into the ground. I remember saying oh shit, oh shit I'm dead. When the bomb hit it was almost like there was no air or sound for about five seconds. Then it blew the ever loving piss out of them. There were flames and smoke and shrapnel flying everywhere. The sound was so loud it made my ears ring. The ground felt like it lifted up and dropped back down. I could actually feel the vibration from the bomb hit my body. Believe it or not, just a couple of minutes after the bomb drop the NVA started to advance again. We were able to fight them back once again, however; we were getting chopped up by their machine gun fire. There was a Marine next to me that stood up for some reason, maybe he just had enough. He was firing his M16 and the spent shells were flying out and dropping on me. One shell hit me on the neck and burned the hell out of me. I turned over just as a round hit him in the side of the neck. It wasn't a bad wound, it just grazed him, but that was enough for him to jump back on the ground again. Here came another F4 phantom. This time he dropped napalm. They must have been the same F4's hitting the top of hill 875. This time the NVA stopped their advance. The battle was over. The NVA pulled back and then they were gone.

We started calling in medivacs for the wounded and then for the dead. Some of the guy's got a little sick when they had to stack body parts in a pile. I was glad I didn't have to do it. My recon team was ordered to scout the area for information as to which direction the NVA was headed and to take a body count. The ground where the napalm hit was still smoking and there where small fires here and there. The napalm smell was still in the air and there were lots of burnt bodies everywhere. We came to a bomb crater that looked like the place where the five hundred pound bomb hit. It looked to be about twenty feet wide and eight feet deep. There were bodies all around the crater along with arms, legs and heads. It truly looked like HELL on earth. I remember thinking, was I ever going to get use to seeing these kinds of things without going out of my head. The brain can only take so much and I was dam close to being there. I started thinking that maybe I should have gone home instead of re-upping to stay. Then I thought about Suki. If I had gone home I would have never met her. I had another thirteen months to do, so I would just have to get with it. There were Marines who had seen and gone through a lot more than me. They lived through it and so would I.

The 9th spent the next four days running patrols by day and setting up ambushes at night from about four hundred meters west of where we ran into the 968th NVA. Thanksgiving came and went almost unnoticed. By the 25th of November we returned to Dong Ha. After a few days we returned to our normal OP (outpost) duty every other day until the middle of December. It was then that the 26th Marines and my recon team were sent to Quang Tri City in the Quang Tri Province. Quang Tri City was in central Vietnam, the major city of Quang Tri Province.

CHAPTER 28

TURNING POINT

Quang Tri was very close to the DMZ (demilitarized zone.) The DMZ was an area that separated the North from South. This happened at the end of the First Indochina War in 1954. The DMZ was intended to be an area free of arms. However, during the Vietnam War (1959-1975), the area around the DMZ was so devastated by fighting that the city probably still bears the effects of it today. The people of Quang Trí were poor because many farmers couldn't use their land for fear of land mines. The farming that did exist was almost wholly for subsistence. Much of the surrounding land was deforested because of the carpet bombing and chemical agents dropped. During the Vietnam War Quang Tri was the site of several fierce battles, in particular the Easter Offensive of 1972. After North Vietnamese troops took the area, the Province was bombed daily by as many as forty bombers, each carrying several tons of bombs. South Vietnamese forces did eventually re-gain the city but lost at least five thousand troops in the process. Quang Tri Province was the scene of some of the fiercest ground fighting of the American war, especially from 1966 to the end of the war in 1975 and was subjected to the heaviest bombing campaign in the history of the world. At the war's end in 1975, the entire province was devastated and most of the population had evacuated. Quang Tri Town at that time, the Province capital and Dong Ha Town were both destroyed.

Not a single building remained standing or useable. Of the some three thousand villages scattered throughout the province, only about eleven remained at the end of the war. The intense bombing, combined with the use of the Agent Orange defoliant, turned the land into a dirt pile with only a fraction of the original triple canopy jungle forest remaining after the war. There were American and South Vietnamese military bases and outposts all over the Province and along the DMZ. Some of the more famous battle sites from the sea coast to the mountains included Dong Ha, LZ Russell, Hill 126, Camp Carroll, Khe Sanh, Hill 881North and South, Con Thien and of course Mutter Ridge where I was wounded for the third and final time.

We were running squad size patrols by day and ambushes at night. We ran eight man recon patrols every other day. Some recon patrols at night. On night patrols I got to use the battery powered night vision scope, we called it star light, star bright. The scope magnified the light of the moon and stars to provide night time vision. It was then on December 15th 1967 when my world turned upside down. We were on a day patrol around 0900 (9AM) moving toward the East. We had a fourteen man squad, I was the radioman. We were in a side by side formation about three to four meters apart in an open field when we came to a rice paddy. Benny and I were only about three meters (nine and a half feet) apart so that we could talk. Benny stepped up on a dike next to a rice paddy. He hollered oh fuck! Vinny, something clicked under my foot. I didn't get a chance to say anything when all of a sudden there was a blast. Benny had stepped on a Bouncing Betti which was the nick name for a jumping mine.

The bouncing betti was an anti personnel mine designed to be used in open areas. Once it was tripped a small propelling charge launches the body of the mine three to four feet into the air. Then the main charge bursts and sprays shrapnel at waist height. There was a common misconception about the mine. Benny and I both thought that it wouldn't detonate until its victim stepped off the trigger. That was a fallacy, just more propaganda. The mine would detonate whether the trigger was released or not. Standing still or attempting to run from the mine would be equally dangerous. The most effective way to survive the mine's detonation would be to fall to the ground laying face down as quickly as possible. The mine had caught him in the inside right leg and blew out his stomach. The blast blew him through the air about five feet and he landed on his knees. He was screaming for me to help him as I ran over to him. I didn't even stop to think that I might step on one too. All I was thinking was that my best friend in the world needed me. I dropped my radio and fell to my knees in front of him. He was screaming so loud and he was in so much pain, that my body started to shake all over. He was trying to keep his intestines from coming out. I pushed my hands against his, only lifting them long enough to grab more of his intestines and tried to shove them back in. He was so blown up I couldn't even recognize what was his leg from his stomach. He started asking for his Mom, it was then I knew he wasn't going to make it. I started screaming oh God, oh God. Doc Billy was on his way over to us from about fifty yards away, but by the time he got there it was too late. Benny just looked at me and laid his head on my lap. I started screaming again oh God not Benny, please

God not my friend. All I could do was look up toward the sky and ask God to spare him, but my prayer wasn't answered. When Doc got there he checked Benny's pulse and said he's gone. I had his blood all over my face, my hands and my arms.

The one thing that went through my mind at that moment was that I never took the time to tell him that I loved him like a brother. Why do men have such a problem telling other men or women how much they care? Doc thought I was hit because there was so much blood all over me. I told him I wasn't hit. Benny had taken almost all of the blast. I started crying, I couldn't even call in his medivac. Cpl. Cain had to do it. He knew how much we liked each other and sometimes called us the twins. Cpl. Cain thought it would be best if I didn't stay in the field. I think he thought I might go into shock or something. I was so angry I yelled at him that I was fine, let's go. We changed our direction after marking the area to be checked for mines by our company Engineers. Even today I don't know for sure if I was in shock or not, I just knew that from that day on I wanted to kill as many VC and NVA that I could. "Hell" if God didn't care about Benny dieing, then I didn't care about God. That's the day I stopped being a Catholic, I wasn't going to make it to heaven anyway, so fuck it. I some how got through the patrol although I felt like I was in a fog.

Later that night I just wanted to be alone. I sat all by myself and cried again for my friend. I made up my mind that night I would never allow myself to ever be close or to love again. I thought about Benny and his poor Mom. It was getting close to Christmas and she would always remember her son died around that time of the year.

How can a Mother ever get over loosing a child? Benny was such a great person. I started feeling a little sorry for myself because now, I was all alone. I had no one now. I didn't want to be here without him. I looked at the Red Rider coin that I had around my neck. I had it ever since I was nine years old. I had sent away for it with two cereal box tops and fifty cents that took me months to save up for. I hung it around my neck for luck when I found out I was going to Vietnam. I thought about giving it to Benny for a Christmas gift. I was going to put it in his Christmas stocking that year. I wondered if I had given it to him sooner that maybe he would still be here. I thought about a lot of thing's that night. That night was the longest night of my life. I still have that coin today. Every Christmas Eve I put it on, go outside and drink a toast to Benny and to the fallen Marines that have died over the years defending our county. I'll never forget him.

Chapter 29

Hue City

Through out the next day and for weeks to come I was in a daze. Nothing seemed to matter anymore. Christmas came and went as well as the New Year. By the third week of January 1968 my recon team was reassigned to the 2nd Battalion 5th Marines Fox Company. They where getting ready to enter Hue City. During the lunar New Year holiday of Tet, a very important week long holiday celebrated all over Vietnam. The Viet Cong and the North Vietnamese Army launched a massive assault on South Vietnam. They seized the American embassy in Saigon. They also seized the city of Hue and its population of about 110,000 citizens. This Tet Offensive began on January 31, 1968.

In the early hours of February 1, 1968, 2nd Platoon of Fox Company and our recon team entered the city and we were under fire. Some units were pinned down along with two Marine tanks by the NVA (North Vietnamese Army) defending a street called Tran Cao Van Street. The Battle of Hue lasted four weeks and cost one hundred and forty American lives. Marines of the First and Fifth Regiments, fighting along side the Army of the Republic of Vietnam's 1st Division was supported by the American Army 7th and 12th Cavalry Regiments. The Marines immediately launched a counter offensive called Operation Hue City. North Vietnamese and Viet Cong forces were driven out of Hue little by little as The Marines retook the city one block at a time fighting house to house.

The Marines retook the Treasury building, the University, the Hospital, the Provincial Headquarters and finally, the Citadel. On February 26, 1968, the city of Hue was declared secure. U.S. forces remained another week to ensure the city's safety and the battle became a big American victory. I wrote about it in my diary even though my recon team was there for only a week. We were transferred to Khe Sanh Hill 558 on the 5th of February to support the Marines 2nd Battalion 26th Regiment.

CHAPTER 30

KHE SANH

Late in January 1968 an element of the 26th regiment was dispatched to the Khe Sanh area where it participated in Operation Scotland. There under the operational control of the 26th, the Marines of 1/9 joined three battalions of the 26th Marine Regiment, to hold the besieged Khe Sanh Combat Base as North Vietnamese soldiers firing from artillery bases at Co Roc, across the Laotian border. The NVA fired thousands of shells into Khe Sanh daily. When we got to Khe Sanh it seemed like there was mass confusion. We where transported to Hill 558 which was about one half mile from the combat base. We had to dig trenches right away and remove elephant grass to make a killing zone about sixty meters completely around the perimeter. Then we had to string concertina barbed wire, better known as the Devils rope around the entire killing zone area along with land mines, leaving only areas that we could run patrols out of. By the time we were completed with the killing zone the Khe Sanh base was reaching a record number of incoming rounds taken in a day 1,307. Most rounds came in when a plane or chopper came in or if the NVA spotters up on Hill 1015 would see a large group of marines standing together.

The Marines at the combat base adopted a technique called the Khe Sanh shuffle, which is a way of quickly moving about in the open, staying alert and then taking cover when the rockets came in. The NVA, although we didn't know at the time, was constructing a trench system that was reaching near the perimeter of the combat base. All the shelling at Khe Sanh left the base a big mess; the air reeked of the trash fires that were everywhere. Some of the rockets hit the ammunition dump, this happened more than once. One time the explosion killed a number of Marines that were standing close to the dump. By late February there were B-52 air strikes, some as close as one and a half miles from base perimeter. The jungle and the elephant grass was tore to bits in some places.

We were on patrol the last week of February from Hill 558, with a platoon searching for the enemy that was shooting mortar rounds daily at the Southeast perimeter of the combat base. We ran into a platoon size NVA ambush and we were chewed up badly. We had heavy fire from both our right and left flanks. We had so many casualties in the first fifteen seconds that we had to withdraw under fire. We were forced to leave our dead. We lost twenty-three Marines and had to recover there their bodies later. When we did recover them they had been mutilated by the NVA. There were a few dead NVA soldiers as well. I was so crazy fucking mad by then that I cut one ear off two of them. I wasn't the only one that did. It's something today that I'm not very proud of, but who knows what they would do in the same circumstance.

CHAPTER 31

HILL 861

In early March the 1st platoon of Delta Co. was hit with mortar rounds at the Khe Sanh base perimeter followed by an attack by the NVA, but the Marines fought them back. Around the same time a USAF C-123 was shot down by a NVA rocket and forty-eight Marines died. Due to the air strip at Khe Sanh being under attack the planes couldn't land, they could only touch down, open the doors and slide the equipment, food and water out on the runway and then take off as fast as they could. Some of the planes didn't make it and were blown up on the air strip killing all on board. Supplies started running out as well as the food and water because of the rocket firing on choppers that tired to deliver the food and water. They were getting blown out of the sky. The combat base, Hill 558 and Hill 861 had to start rationing the food and water. We were down to one meal a day and one cup of water. The Khe Sanh base took around one thousand one hundred rounds by the third week of March.

By the third week of March we started getting radio intercepts and other intelligence that the NVA has started to pull out some of its major units. The 9th and 26th Marines started to attack NVA fortified positions South East of the combat base and by using supporting arms were able to clear the trench line and bunkers of NVA. We were able to kill over one hundred of the bastards; I was pleased although it still wasn't enough to satisfy me, I was still dam mad about Benny being killed. Also during this time two NVA divisions were destroyed. More than ten thousand NVA were estimated to be killed during the battle of Khe Sanh, mostly by B-52's and artillery attacks. While the NVA divisions were tied up at Khe Sanh trying to over run the combat base, Hill 558 and 861, they weren't able to attack Quang Tri City or Hue City during the Tet Offensive. That was the NVA Generals intended goal during Tet. Instead of joining that fight a large portion of their troops were tied down and eventually destroyed at Khe Sanh. When they eventually tried to move some of their troops to Hue City, it was too little and too late.

On April 1st Operation Pegasus, the relief of Khe Sanh started. This operation was commanded by the US Army and involved both Army and Marine units that approached from the east. On April 5th my recon team along with the 2nd Battalion 26th Marines, were still holding Hills 558 and 861 west of the combat base. Marines from 2/26 Golf Co were instructed to patrol a North-South ridge line about two thousand meters west of Hill 558. The company departed Hill 558 at 0700 and approached the crest of Hill 861 at about 1100. Before reaching the crest of the ridge Golf Co came under heavy enemy fire and was pinned down through out the afternoon, but was able to with draw back to Hill 558 before sundown. They brought out their wounded and two of their dead, but were forced to leave eight Marines on the battlefield. They were surrounded by the NVA. Air and artillery strikes were called in to cover their withdrawal. The Commanding Officer of 2/26 proposed and the Regimental Commander approved a two-pronged assault of the ridgeline. My recon team was assigned to Fox Company. We departed Hill 558 before first light in order to arrive at a line of departure north of the ridgeline. Golf 2/26 departed Hill 558 at first light in hopes of distracting the enemy from us and our movement to position for an assault from the East side of the ridge. Although the attack was planned for 1200, circumstances prevented the two companies from getting into position before 1400. On command Golf Company was attacking into the enemy's line while we and Fox Co were flanking an attack from the North. We were able to roll up their line. The Northern two-thirds of the enemy positions were captured with the NVA withdrawing toward the Southern end of the ridge. At that point we were strung out along several hundred meters of the ridgeline and Golf was not able to complete an up hill assault against the Southern end of the ridgeline before nightfall.

Although 2/26 wanted to leave both companies in position through the night, permission was refused and once again we and the two companies with drew to Hill 558, again forced to leave some of our dead behind. Once again air and artillery fires blanketed the ridgeline. A battalion attack which included Echo Co, Fox, Hotel, and Golf companies was planned for the 10th and was executed as scheduled. When we reached the top of the ridgeline we met little resistance. The NVA had abandoned their positions and retreated into the jungles to the west. On April 5th 1968 the 76 day siege was officially declared ended. Since 7,000 North Vietnamese were still reported to be in the vicinity of Khe Sanh the end of the siege was more official than real. The North Vietnamese had fired more than 40,000 artillery, rocket and mortar rounds into the Khe Sanh combat base during the siege. The enemy had failed to take the base and had lost thousand's of soldiers in the process. For our part in this action, the 9th, 26th, and my recon team received the Presidential Unit Citation.

Following the fierce fighting after the break out at Khe Sanh, the regiment began conducting operations around the Rock pile and Vandergrift Combat Base where we met with heavy resistance. The first of these operations was Operation Lancaster II which was a major 9th Marines multi-regimental helicopter assault. During this operation the Marines captured several 75mm pack howitzers which had been firing at Camp Carroll. After Khe Sanh, the 26th Marines 1st and 3rd battalions were transferred to Quang Tri Base. The 2nd Battalion 26th Regiment (2/26) Marines were placed under the operational control of the 4th Marines. This was at the end of May. My recon team stayed attached to 2/26. The 4th Marines were going to sea on the USS Princeton and the USS Dubuque.

The USS Princeton took on Echo and Fox Company of 2/26 and my recon team along with Golf and Hotel companies were assigned to the USS Dubuque. She was a LPD 8 amphibious assault ship that carried amphibious assault vehicles for beach landings. The USS Princeton was being used to bring Marines in for aerial assaults on helicopters, while we hit the beaches on the assault vehicles from the USS Dubuque. Cpl Cain and Berry were now the only guys I really could talk too now. Reed had received his orders to go home, his tour was over. He didn't go with us when we left Hill 558; he was transported to Da Nang. I never really got close to him like I did with Benny, but I was going to miss him. I was happy he was going home.

CHAPTER 32

ON BOARD

Life on board a ship was something I had no idea was going to be so great. The food on board was so good after eating C-rations month after month. We actually had hammocks to sleep in. No day patrols, no night ambushes. The Navy even had cinnamon buns and coffee for breakfast along with eggs and ham. We spent most of the day cleaning our weapons, writing home and doing a lot of PT (physical training) while the Navy guys watched us run around the deck of the ship trying to stay fit. They would look at us and just shake their heads. I'm sure they thought what a bunch of dumb asses. I got to know a couple of them and they were pretty cool guys. They had worried looks on their faces when we had to leave the ship and go into combat. One of the things's that struck fear into me and the other Marines was when the horn would go off. That meant we had to run to our barracks as fast as we could and get out of the way of the sailors. They would lock down the doors and we had to stay there until they opened them again. I thought about old movies that I saw when I was young and remembered how sailors got trapped in the ship when it went down, of course the chances of that happening was zero, but I still thought about it.

We ran beach landings between Dong Hoi, Dong Ha and Quang Tri. There were two major operations while we were aboard ship. They were Operation Scotland II and Nevada. Hitting the beach wasn't like in the WWII movies although on my first beach landing that's what went through my head. I could see myself getting shot while I tried to get to the beach and not drowning in the process. There were a few shoots fired when we hit the beach and a few guys did get wet because of being to far out in the water when we landed, but no one drowned and there were very few wounds. Most of the battles took place when we traveled inland from the beach. We only stayed out in the bush for a few days at a time and then we were brought back aboard the ship. We were being used as an amphibious ready group. Ready to go in where ever there was a hot spot and support enforcement was needed. We were off and on the ship through the months June, July, and August. There were some fire fights here and there, but for the most part they were small ones, if you can call a fire fight small. Nothing seems small when you're being shot at.

We did lose some Marines during the operations. On one patrol we lost an entire squad when they were ambushed while trying to cross a river. We had to recover their bodies down the river about a mile. It took us two days to find all of them. One other thing that happened that I will never forget was on a night patrol to setup an ambush. It was around 2200 hours (10pm) when we reached the location for the ambush. We had just moved into our positions when all of a sudden a M79 grenade launcher was fired off and then all hell broke loose. I could hear and see the rounds firing through the air from M16's and AK47's as well as a BAR (Browning automatic rifle that fires a 30-06 round.) The last Marine in our ambush had sat down next to a NVA that was about six feet away from him and sitting on the tail end of their ambush. It was so dam dark you couldn't see more than five feet in front of you. Well when our man sat down he wondered who was next to him because he thought he was on the end of our ambush, so he asked whose there. The answer he got back was not in English. He fired off a round in the direction of the voice with his M79 grenade launcher. That's when the air filled with bullets. Surprisingly none of our guy's got hit, but two NVA's bit the dust. One had his head almost taken off by the M79 round and the other got it in the back with a M16 round.

Chapter 33

Alone

On the 24th of June 1968 four days after my birthday my world would be turned up side down once again. We were on a five mile patrol around Quang Tri. I was standing next to Cpl Cain, SSgt Henry, Berry, a couple of scouts, a dog handler and his scout dog, a German Sheppard. We were looking at a spider trap at the foot of some trees. They were talking about what to do next about the trap, blow it up or send a tunnel rat (a small Marine) down to look around, to see if there was a tunnel leading to some where. I had just walked away over to where the dog was when the dog barked and took off running dragging the dog handler with him. I didn't know what was going on, but I ran like a lion was after me. By this time the dog handler was up and running. The dog heard rounds coming in from a distance. He saved me and the dog handler that day. Two 40mm rounds hit right in the middle of them. The rounds were friendly fire. The blast knocked me down and when I got up I looked back and saw a cloud of smoke. I could hear screaming but couldn't see anything. All of a sudden Berry came running out of the cloud of smoke screaming. He had smoke coming from his back and I thought he was on fire. I dropped my radio and ran after him to knock him down on the ground so I could put out the fire.

"Well" he wasn't on fire, a gas grenade had exploded on his combat belt and gas was shooting out of the top of it.

When I reached him the gas hit me in the face. Anyone who has ever experienced tear gas in the face knows that when it hits you, that's all she wrote. My eyes went shut and tears started falling, my nose started running and my face stung like it was on fire. I lost my breath for a few seconds. Finally I could breathe again and although my face was still stinging I was able to see again. I tried to put some water on my face, but it didn't help much. I was sure that there were wounded so I ran over and put my radio back on. This would be a day that I never will forget for as long as I live. When the smoke cleared away I was horrified from what I saw. The dog handler and the dog made it out of the blast zone as well as I did, but everyone else standing there was hit with the shrapnel. I saw a guy sitting down with wounds from head to foot. His name was Sgt Cosby. The two scouts were hit. One had just both of his big toes blown off and that was it, I couldn't believe it. The other scout lost his right leg just below the knee; it was hanging on by a small piece of skin. He was sitting up on the ground and when he saw his leg he grabbed it, looked at it and said FUCK they blew my God Dam leg off. Then he threw it back down on the ground. One of the Corpsman was there trying to bandage his leg.

Other Marines were working on the other scout and Berry who had wounds but small ones. I was so happy he was OK. He was medivaced out but returned after a few days. I heard someone yell that I was fucked up because I was looking around sort of in a daze. Sgt Cosby told him that I was fine. Then he told me to call in for medivac. I called Hotel Company and asked for medivac and started giving them the medivac numbers of the wounded. That's when I found out that Cpl Cain had been hit. I ran over to where he was and I almost went into shock. There was Doc Billy the corpsman, working on Cpl Cain along with another Marine. I think his name was Steve, I didn't know him very well. Doc kept saying to Cpl Cain while he was working on him, don't die on me, "dam it" please Tristan. They were friends just like Benny and me. The medivac helicopter took about twenty minutes to get there. Cpl Cain (Tristan) was literally torn in half and died on the trip back to the base hospital. I wanted to scream at the top of my lungs, why "God" why. Cpl Cain was the greatest Marine that I have ever known. Years later I would find his name on the Vietnam Veterans Memorial Wall. After all the wounded were medivaced we found SSgt Henry. He was hit as bad as Tristan, but he was killed instantly. I tried to keep my emotions inside, but I couldn't believe that everyone I liked and loved was now gone, Benny, Reed, and now Tristan. Now, I was all alone, except for Berry and I wasn't going to let him get close to me. I never have again, ever since Benny.

CHAPTER 34

MUTTERS RIDGE

We spent the next couple of weeks running patrols out of Quang Tri. It was mid July when we headed back aboard the USS Dubuque. We stayed aboard the ship for the next month. I wrote in my diary about the things that I had seen and felt over the last few weeks. This would be the last entry in my diary. I sent home what I had written up till then. I knew I was getting real close to the end of my tour, so I was happy when rumor had it that we were going to Okinawa and that some of us were going to be replaced by new Marines. It wasn't to be. Since I wasn't able to put down what happened in my diary in September 1968, the rest of my story is from memory. I have tried to be as accurate as possible.

I was lying down on my hammock when a platoon sergeant named Sgt Little came in and told all of us to saddle up we have a mission. We were going to a place called Mutter Ridge Nui Cay Tri in South Vietnam. Mutter Ridge was connected by several high spots one of which was Hill 461. The 3rd Marines who were on Hill 461 had run into a battalion of NVA that were camped around the ridge. I just looked up at him and said nothing. He couldn't mean all of us, hell I only had one week left to go. He did mean ALL of us. He looked at me and said that means you too. When I told him I was a short timer he said I don't give a dam how short you are, you're going! This was September 14th. I guess I should have been glad at the time to get off the ship. We had just gone through a terrible typhoon and we were locked down for a couple of days. No one could even eat because we were so sick from the swaying of the ship so much. We were going to hit the beach and then go inland to an area to meet up with the rest of the companies off the USS Princeton. They were being choppered in.

After we meet up with the rest of the battalion. We all boarded helicopters and were flown in to a place called LZ (landing zone) Margo. LZ Margo was a primary fire base. This was going to be a large operation around what they called the rock pile. LZ Margo had allot of trees that had to be blown away so that the helicopters could land. My recon team ran about a two hour recon patrol almost immediately after landing. It was really hilly and wet. The jungle was very dense. On our patrol we found a path built in the side of the hill with stairs made from bamboo with hand rails. We found a couple of bunkers that were empty, however; it was a sure sign that the NVA was in the area. When we returned from our patrol I saw a NVA solider down on his knees with his hands tried around his back. This is hard to believe but apparently one of the guys in a gun team had taken a little stroll to see if he could find some water from the bamboo trees. We setup sort of a perimeter and had some security when we got to the top of the hill. Anyway he had gone for a little walk, but he had left his M16. He came back about ten minutes later and he had this NVA soldier with him. The only thing he took with him was his K-Bar (a combat knife) and he had this NVA soldier at knifepoint. Everyone was amazed that he captured a NVA soldier with only a knife. This NVA soldier had a weapon with him and everything else they carry into combat. So if he wanted to he could have killed him on the spot. I think he just really wanted to surrender to us. I remember a helicopter coming in and taking him out right away for intelligence, but the interrupter did find out a couple of thing's that gave me the cold chills, one of which was that my recon team had walked right through their ambush but they never opened up on us. I guess it was because they wanted to remain hidden until night fall. Hell, I really don't know but I'm glad they didn't. We only had six men on our patrol. They flew him out around 1300(1:00pm) in the afternoon. I remember them getting back to us later that day after they had interrogated him and he had told them that we were surrounded by a regiment of North Vietnamese soldiers. So we set up a perimeter based on the information we received. It was dark, it was raining, it was cold and I couldn't see my hand in front of my face.

A couple of listening post of four guys each was sent out about thirty meters from the perimeter line. They were there to listen incase there was any movement toward our positions. If anything was heard then they would radio back to one of our radioman that was on radio watch. They could give him the information which could be how many NVA soldiers they thought might be moving into a position. Also to let us know that they (the LP) were coming back in so that we didn't fire on them.

It was around 2330 hours (11:30pm) when I had taken over radio watch from Berry. Berry laid down behind me to get a little sleep. I thought I could hear the NVA walking through the jungle from time to time and every once in a while I thought I heard a twig break. The hill that we were on had a stream down below it and it may have actually been part of the stream that ran through LZ Margo. I thought I could hear NVA walking through it. I couldn't tell if I actually was hearing anything or if I was imagining it. I whispered on the radio mic to the LP and asked if they were hearing anything. I didn't get back an answer right away so I just listened for a minute. Finally the LP transmitted back to me that they were hearing movement. I couldn't hear a sound. It was almost like I had lost my hearing. My heart was pounding and sweat started pouring down my face along with the rain. I thought to myself how could I be sweating, it was so cold. A moment later I heard a pop, pop, pop, pop and crack, crack, crack. It was from M16's and AK47's. The LP had opened up on the NVA. The LP called in telling me that they were coming back in with one wounded and that they had to leave one dead Marine behind. I was with Hotel Co. 2nd platoon and received a call from Hotel Co. 3rd platoon that the NVA had made contact on their right flank and were breaching their perimeter. The 2nd Lieutenant of 2nd platoon ran over to me and grabbed my radio transmitter. He was calling the 3rd platoon CP (command post) to find out the situation. The 3rd platoon CP said that their perimeter zone had been breached and that they were falling back to meet up with 2nd platoon. The NVA started shooting 82mm mortar rounds; I could hear them drop in the tube, "thoomp." That was the sound they made like a thumping noise and then they made a whirring noise. It's a distinct sound a mortar round make when it comes in. You could hear them coming in and you knew that they were going to be close. A couple of them fell close to us. I heard a scream and when I looked I saw Berry. He had been hit in the

head with shrapnel, he died in seconds. The 2nd Lieutenant said lets go and I was up following him down a
make shift path. I heard the 2nd LT tell the 1st Lieutenant of Hotel Co that we were being over run and that we
needed artillery. I heard screaming and shouting along
with M16's and AK47's going off. More mortar rounds
went off and I could see some of the North Vietnamese
soldiers now. It was really strange, but we ran by some
of them and they didn't seem to see us. We were only
about ten feet away from them. It was dark and raining so
"Hell" I'm sure the LT saw them, but was to busy to care.

Finally the LT stopped, handed me the transmitter
and gave me the order to call in artillery. I wasn't sure
where on the grid map we were anymore because we
ran so far, but how far! We could have been outside the
perimeter line by now. I called in the artillery, 105mm
rounds. Within minutes the first four rounds came in,
one, two, three and four. Right away I knew we were in
trouble. The rounds were close, the ground shook and
dirt flew in the air. The LT turned around and said lets go
back. I still have no idea to this day why he went in the
direction he did, unless he was trying to meet up with the
3rd platoon. We had traveled about twenty meters when
we saw a corpsman yelling for help. He was working on
a Marine that had one arm blown off; he was trying to
stop the bleeding. The corpsman was bleeding also. He
had been hit in the back just under his flax jacket. It was
a bad wound, but he was trying to help the Marine from
going into shock. The LT grabbed up the Marine over his
shoulder and I grab the corpsman by his arm pits and
started dragging him out of the open. I couldn't pick him
up with my radio so this was the best way to move him.

While I was doing this, the next four 105mm rounds came in. The first round hit and it was close. I was down on one knee trying to cover me and the corpsman. After the second round hit I felt the dirt and the blast wave from it, I got up and started dragging him again.

When the third round came in it was loud and I knew it was really going to be close. The air went heavy and the round stopped making the whirring noise they make when they hit. When a round goes quiet then you know you're really fucked. That's exactly what I said "FUCK". When the round hit I felt like a one ton weight had hit me in the side of my body. The blast through me in the air and I hit a tree upside down. I landed on my head and my helmet broke my nose and my front teeth when I hit the ground. My helmet was stuck on part of my face and I couldn't get it off right away. When I did I reached back and felt my leg. All I got was a hand full of skin and blood. I screamed that my leg was blow off, but actually my thigh had been torn away from the bone, and my knee cap was gone. I had small pieces of shrapnel in my side, neck, and head. I had lost my navicular bone in my right wrist and my right ear had been torn at the top next to my head.

I was a mess and even though I should have been in lots of pain I didn't feel a thing. I could see from all the blood on my hands that my face was tore up but I had no idea of how bad. I was starting to go into shock so I kept shaking my head and telling myself, your fine, your fine. That's when I realized that my teeth were broken and my upper lip was spilt. I looked up for the wounded corpsman but I couldn't see him anywhere. What I did see was three or four NVA soldiers running by, about five meters from me. Then a couple more of them came running by. I found my 45 cal lying next to me and picked it up. That's when I realized that my right hand didn't work right due to the wound. I had to change to my left hand to fire. I fired off four or five shots before I was on empty. I couldn't re-load my magazine so I started picking up the rounds and throwing them at the soldiers making a bang noise like a little kid playing cowboys and Indians. One of them even looked at me, but kept on running. To this day I have no idea of what he thought, but he didn't shoot at me.

Next thing I knew I was picked up and dragged down a path and thrown next to a pile of Marines and a couple of NVA soldiers. It was the 2nd Lieutenant that dragged me there. That would be the last time I would ever see him. There were corpsman attending the wounded and he gave me a shot of morphine. I was just starting to feel the pain so I was glad to get it. He yelled in my ear that I was going home. I asked about my leg and he said its fine you'll be up walking around in no time. Of course he lied, but that was a good thing. Better to think your fine than to know the truth right away.

The NVA had retreated because of the artillery. I was told by another Marine helping out with the wounded that a radio call was made and the incoming artillery fire stopped. I was dam glad. I didn't want to get hit again. The morphine did the job. I was out like a light. It wasn't until the next day that I can remember coming out of it for a few minutes. Just long enough to hear that the jungle was so dense that they wouldn't be able to land the medivac helicopters. So the helicopters came in, hovered and they lifted me and all the other wounded fifty feet in the air. I only remember being pulled up on a cable and into the helicopter and then I passed out again. I was in and out of it, sometimes knowing what was happening around me, like when we landed in the rear and I was taken to the hospital.

CHAPTER 35

INNOCENCE

I remember when they were cutting off my uniform, my dog tags and my watch. The corpsman that cut off my watch showed it to me, smiled and said hay look! it took a licking but it's still ticking. I was wearing a Timex combat watch. That's the last thing I remembered for days. They were running out of blood plasma when we got hit in the field due to so many wounded. They had to give me a small amount of a different type than mine and it caused my body temperature to go up and down between 103 and 105 degs. In the hospital they poured some kind of liquid over me and I had cotton covering my entire body, even my forehead to bring down my temperature. I remember coming out of it again long enough to be aware it. I also remember the Battalion Sergeant Major telling me that they got hit again on the 16th on the ridge and at LZ Margo. He told me that I was lucky to get out when I did. It was a blood bath. That was the last thing I really remember for a week.

I woke up a week later in Japan at an Army Hospital. I remember talking to a doctor and he said you're going home. The war's over for you. I just thought, "Wow! It's over." I was going home. I didn't know at the time if I would loose my leg or not, but I was going home. The time I spent in Vietnam has left its mark on me in more ways than I can count. The thing's I saw, the thing's I did, the thing's I felt, would be with me for the rest of my life.

I guess I would be concerned if it didn't. If I could just shrug it off then I would be more concerned. I would think that maybe something was really wrong with me. I lost the guy's that were close to me over there. I had also lost something else that I could never again get back. I had lost my innocence.

Because of my time as a Marine in Vietnam I have had or may have some of the following… effects of Agent Orange, nightmares, cancer, marriage breakup, or feel suicidal. But I also have a chance to change some of these. The most difficult memory to forget will be the sound of helicopter blades. Whenever I hear the sound of a helicopter I see the jungle. The sound is very distinctive and strikes more memories than anything else. As for the Hollywood movies that seemed to be made in abundance about the Vietnam War, there is only one movie that I have seen that comes close to showing what it was like. That movie is Platoon.

The most difficult part to accept about the Vietnam War wasn't the war itself, but the fact that no one in the United States seemed to care. One day we were 18 and 19 year olds living in a hot humid jungle full of every bug in the world that could bite, looking for an enemy who we were trained to kill and having the capability to kill people using what ever means possible and not having to answer for it. Carrying the most efficient weapons the United States Government could provide. Flying around in gun ships or riding on tanks and in APC's. Clearing bunkers, blowing up unexploded bombs, living and sleeping with a loaded weapon twenty-four hours a day and where most of the rules of a normal life that we had been brought up with, simply did not apply.

I was lucky because I was wounded over there and in the hospital for a very long time. I had a chance to get my head on straight before retuning to the real world, with no jungle, no war and no weapons. It was like being on another planet. I was out of sync with my own country! But instead of a kind word or a welcome home, we were all treated with abuse, sarcasm and contempt. Where if you defended yourself or touch someone you could be charged with assault, where we had to immediately adjust to a new set of rules. If we were seen in our uniform we were looked down on as if we were criminals. Where no one was even slightly interested in saying "What was it like?" or "We're glad that you're back" and where we were expected to simply forget about our experiences as if they never happened. Where we were never mention it again and go back to a normal life. When I came back there was no band, no crowds and no welcome. The only people there were my close relatives to drive me home.

This is not by far the worst story of the Vietnam War, to this day not very many people care, not many people are interested, not many people ever ask. The war for each soldier may only have been one or two short years of their life, but it is without doubt the most memorable and to return to your own country to be abused, ignored, looked down upon and forgotten is a most shameful thing.

Since returning from Vietnam I have only come across a few people who are interested in asking what it was like. I don't usually tell anyone I was in Vietnam unless it comes up in a conversation or someone asks.

I didn't start out to write a book, I just needed to sit down and put some of my thoughts down in the hope that it would help me find my way. I wanted to share this with the people I care and love so much. God bless the ones who have stuck by me for all of these years. Maybe now the nightmares will end.

The End

Epilog

After spending more than a year at the Bremerton Navel Hospital in Washington State, I returned to active duty with the Marine Corps. While I was still recovering from the wounds I had received in Vietnam, I continued to pursue my career as a Warrant Officer in the Marine Corps. Unfortunately I was unable to recover enough to continue my service and was medically retired with full benefits.

After a few years of going to college while working at different jobs I was able to find employment with a major aircraft company in the State of Washington where I have been employed for the last thirty-four years. I was married for twenty years now divorced to which I believe Vietnam played a part. I have two sons and three grandchildren. Although I never regained the total use of my leg and hand I am happy with the out come of both. Over the last forty some years my opinion has changed about Vietnam, but one thing has never changed.

It's my belief that the self-serving anti Vietnam War movement damaged our country beyond measure. In the process they shamelessly denigrated all Americans who fought and died there.

3910450